THE CRUCIBLES THAT SHAPE US

NAVIGATING *the* DEFINING CHALLENGES *of* LEADERSHIP

GAYLE D. BEEBE

FOREWORD BY DAVID BROOKS

An imprint of InterVarsity Press
Downers Grove, Illinois

InterVarsity Press
P.O. Box 1400 | Downers Grove, IL 60515-1426
ivpress.com | email@ivpress.com

InterVarsity Press® is the publishing division of InterVarsity Christian Fellowship/USA®. For more information, visit intervarsity.org.

Scripture quotations, unless otherwise noted, are from The Holy Bible, English Standard Version, copyright © 2001 by Crossway Bibles, a division of Good News Publishers. Used by permission. All rights reserved.

While any stories in this book are true, some names and identifying information may have been changed to protect the privacy of individuals.

The publisher cannot verify the accuracy or functionality of website URLs used in this book beyond the date of publication.

Cover design: David Fassett
Interior design: Jeanna Wiggins
Images: Getty 1208915671, © 4khz / iStock / Getty Images Plus

ISBN 978-1-5140-0806-5 (print) | ISBN 978-1-5140-0808-9 (digital)

Printed in the United States of America ∞

Library of Congress Cataloging-in-Publication Data
A catalog record for this book is available from the Library of Congress.

30   29   28   27   26   25   24 | 12   11   10   9   8   7   6   5   4   3   2   1

To Pam

God's provision for the present, and

To Anna, Liz, and Richard

God's promise for the future

CONTENTS

FOREWORD

DAVID BROOKS

T HERE IS A SCENE DEEP IN THIS BOOK that struck me as one of the keys to understanding the whole. Gayle Beebe is driving around Santa Barbara, near the Westmont College that he leads. There had been fires nearby in the days leading up to that drive, threatening campus and his community, and he is in the car with his daughter, pre-dawn, surveying the situation and trying to see what needs to be done to keep everybody safe. The rain is pouring down.

Gayle reports that as they were cruising the neighborhood, some premonition caused them to turn around and return home. It was a consequential decision, for that was the morning of the mudslides, and Gayle and his daughter might have driven into the grip of the slides that would take so many lives as people were sleeping and caught tragically unawares.

Where did that premonition come from?

It reminds me of the old line that we don't see with our eyes; we see with our whole life. Over the years, if we are curious and really looking, we are building up a storehouse of models in our head, models that give us an intuitive awareness for how things will flow and not flow. These unconscious models give us the ability, as Gayle writes in this book, to "read the air."

This ability is less about conscious calculation than it is a subliminal sense for what things will go together and what things will never go together, which way events will unfold and which way events will not unfold. This kind of knowledge is held mostly unconsciously, but it is built up consciously. It is the accumulation of a life spent reading, observing, and reflecting. It is knowledge transmogrified into wisdom. I once came across a recipe for a Chinese dish that instructed the cook to add an ingredient just before the water was about to boil. How do you know if the water is about to boil if it is not yet boiling? Experience. Wisdom.

I've been fortunate to have the chance to visit Westmont College annually for the past several years. Each time, I get to hear Gayle make a presentation about what he's been thinking about over the previous year, and I get to make a presentation about the thoughts that have been bouncing around in my head for that year. I'm always amazed by how our curiosity runs on parallel tracks.

For example, in 2023, I mentioned that I had become obsessed with the philosophy of Iris Murdoch. Specifically, I was obsessed by the way she links perception and morality. In the normal course of events, she writes, we see other people in self-serving ways, in ways that flatter our egos. Or we see people as instruments to be used to our own ends. But the key to being a good person is to see people as they are, to cast a "just and loving attention" on others, with eyes that are charitable and loving. She doesn't put it this way, but our goal should be to see others a little of the way Jesus sees, with infinite compassion and mercy.

Gayle came up to me afterward and described his long fascination with Murdoch, and his study of her work, earlier in his career. It is amply evident in this book. As you explore its pages, you will see how often Gayle emphasizes the need to see things clearly. We sometimes think leadership is mostly about decision-making and acting. But I would say—and this book confirms the idea—that leadership is first of all the ability to answer this question: What is really going on here?

Gayle asks us to see in the deepest sense. Not only to ask: What events are unfolding, and what events are likely to unfold? But more crucially: Do I see what's happening to me? Do I see what's happening because of me? Do I see around the mental shortcomings that prevent me from really seeing? For example, have I factored in the truth that Daniel Kahneman identified—the reality that what you see is not all there is? There's much more to any person or any situation than is immediately visible, and proper seeing always involves taking the extra step to ask: What am I missing here?

Gayle is writing about crucibles here, those difficult life moments, and you will profit from his taxonomy of crucibles, the way he categorizes crises into different types and helps us understand them more clearly. But I also come away with the awareness that the definition of a crucible, or any crisis, is that it shatters our normal way of seeing. In these moments, because of some tragedy or some betrayal, the normal patterns of life do not pertain. Everything is confusing, in turmoil. The old models don't apply. One has to learn to re-see.

The tragedies that struck Santa Barbara—the fires and the floods—were a set of crucibles. I have been impressed by how they have permanently altered the way the folks at Westmont and perhaps the whole city see each other. There is a greater awareness of vulnerability, amid all the beauty of the place, a greater awareness of mutual dependence, and greater sense of community.

That kind of knowledge is hard won, after much grief, and it is a reminder that wisdom is an intellectual, emotional, and moral category all at once. In this book you will encounter two kinds of wisdom, one prosaic and one sacred. Gayle has read widely and questioned the secular writers who try to understand the world. Like all great teachers he passes along a lot of their wisdom in these pages. But his seeing is always inspired by the One who sees all. Ultimately, we are all trying to cast the kind of attention on some people that Jesus cast on all people. It is an impossible standard but the right one to orient your life around.

This is what all schools, and particularly Westmont, aim at their best to teach. I hope as you read this book, you will grow in your capacity to open your eyes and see.

INTRODUCTION

LESSONS IN ENDURANCE

Let us run with perseverance the race that is set before us.

HEBREWS 12:1

When you're going through hell, keep going.

SIR WINSTON CHURCHILL

THE UNRELENTING RAINFALL BEGAN shortly after 3:00 a.m. on Tuesday, January 9, 2018. An atmospheric river had arrived over Santa Barbara and dumped its total payload in nine minutes. I'd awoken to the sound of pounding rain, and I felt the impact of this violent storm as I wandered out to the kitchen.

Officials had cautioned us about the storm the day before, and we'd also received third-hand reports that several Westmont students who surfed intended to "ride" the asphalt waves two miles downhill to the ocean. I initially found these reports humorous, but as I stood in the kitchen watching the torrential downpour, they terrified me. Thanks be to God, none of our students were awake—or awake enough to grab their surfboards. However, just a few hundred yards to the east of our campus, one of three creek beds that run to the ocean carried a huge wall of water that would ultimately destroy one hundred homes, seriously damage four hundred others, and end the lives of twenty-three people who were crushed or swept away in the debris flow.

Most of those around the world who awoke to the news of the Montecito debris flow read it as just another news story of human tragedy piped in on digital media. But for those of us in harm's way, it came as a demoralizing setback. Just three weeks earlier we had survived the Thomas Fire, a wildfire running the ridgeline of the Santa Ynez Mountains above campus, and one of the largest blazes in California history. It ruined the air quality in Santa Barbara and, after burning for six days, forced the evacuation of our students on December 10, 2017, right before finals week. We had just returned to campus and started spring semester on January 8 when we learned about the impending storm. But none of us could have imagined how bad it would be. Although local officials had issued warnings and even encouraged residents to evacuate, few left their homes.

More than a year after these two disasters, I spoke at a national gathering of college presidents about our emergency preparedness plans. I explained how we'd responded to a natural disaster we'd anticipated (the Thomas Fire) and one no one had expected (the Montecito debris flow). As we moved into the Q and A, my emotional response to one question surprised me: "What have you learned about yourself and about God as a result of these catastrophic events?" Visual memories of people I knew who had died overwhelmed me. As I choked back my emotions, I began sharing all that this season meant to me personally.

THE LESSONS OF CATASTROPHIC EVENTS

At the time of the Montecito debris flow, many people who had previously been evacuated for what turned out to be nonevents chose this time to stay in their homes—with disastrous consequences. I attended seven funerals in thirty days. I felt the loss of many people in the community who had done so much to make life better for others.

I honored local newscasters at our opening convocation on January 8, only to see them a week later suffering from posttraumatic stress disorder because they'd been among the first to discover bodies swept downstream to the ocean.

What, then, did I learn about myself? In the wake of these tragedies, I needed to figure out a way to build meaning from all the discrete pieces of individual information that now needed to be woven into a meaningful whole. This undertaking would be the linchpin motivating my behavior.

As for the second part of the question—what had I learned about God—I realized I'd been thinking about this for a long time. My father had died suddenly and unexpectedly in 1989, just a few years after the abrupt loss of my favorite pastor in 1982. Both of these experiences led to deep soul-searching and had taught me a great deal about the nature of faith, the harsh realities of life, and how our response to tragedy and suffering shapes us. Other setbacks and obstacles I've faced have taught me that life is a perpetual gauntlet with challenge on one side and opportunity on the other—it's never simply one or the other but both at the same time. I've come to rely on God because of these experiences of suffering, not in spite of them.

Despite my challenges, I've developed a deep and abiding confidence in the goodness and grace of God. I have come to see my hardships not as barriers to God, but as divine passageways. Ultimately, I have discovered that my crucibles are the same trials God has used throughout history to challenge and shape his people—but only when they let him.

How, then, do we learn to let him?

THE CRUCIBLES THAT SHAPE US

Harvard business historian Nancy Koehn writes poignantly of this process in her book *Forged in Crisis: The Power of Courageous Leadership in Turbulent Times.* Her book elevates and accents how challenges and crises have remarkable power to shape our lives and forge our leadership. In similar fashion, this book explains how we can learn from the crucibles of life, invite God into the middle of them, and subsequently turn them into triumphs of the human spirit.[1] Crucibles have the power to shape us by refining our character, calling forth our best effort, and teaching us to rely on God. Rarely if ever anticipated, crucibles test our capacity to adapt and change. In turn, they also invite us to find new solutions to vexing problems to secure successful and sustaining outcomes both personally and professionally.

What defines a *crucible* is a modification and combination of the three aspects of the word that *Merriam-Webster* outlines: (1) a high degree of heat or energy that (2) creates a severe or significant test and (3) uses a place, situation, or experience to catalyze growth, refinement, and change. Working from this definition and reflecting on experiences that have shaped me, I explore seven defining crucibles that confront and challenge virtually every leader at some point. We'll cover each one in a chapter of this book.

The crucible of missed meaning. This crucible involves the suffering we experience when our incomplete understanding causes us to miss the meaning in a situation and respond from mistaken perception. Failing to develop self-understanding and self-regulation—two essential ingredients to success in life and leadership—can limit our comprehension and knowledge.

The crucible of enduring challenge. This experience focuses on perseverance and the honest admission that success stems mostly from a firm resolve to keep going rather than give up, despite how much we may know. We conquer persistent challenges by outlasting the obstacles and the opposition and believing fully in our mission and purpose.

The crucible of human treachery. These situations relate primarily to a spiritual and intellectual struggle: How do we handle betrayal? Cultivating deeper self-awareness, a willingness to self-correct, and clarity of purpose help us combat sabotage and betrayal.

The crucible of awakened moral conscience. This crucible recognizes the need for leaders to develop character and integrity. We experience a moral awakening personally when we confront our failure to live up to our deeply held convictions and determine to do better. In 2020, our nation faced a reassessment of how well we honor the promises of our founding ideals and how we can build a more just and equitable society. Or, in the words of Dr. Martin Luther King Jr., how do we pursue the long "arc of the moral universe . . . [that] bends toward justice"?

The crucible of social conflict. This confronts us today. Born of long-simmering social tensions throughout our country, these festering divisions arise from unfulfilled promises activated by social unrest. Recognizing nonviolent, civil disobedience as a biblical imperative has given Christians the spiritual strength to endure hardship and setback, while pursuing the greater good of a free and equitable society. We still have a long way to go, but we cling to hope, which drives all constructive and enduring social change.

The crucible of human suffering. The sixth crucible occurs when we're powerless in the face of natural disaster, disease, or human evil. Navigating such suffering requires a larger context of meaning and purpose, and a caring community. As our community at Westmont experienced dangerous disasters, mourned deaths, and welcomed displaced students fleeing human evil, the grace and faithfulness of God and the love and support of our extended community helped us endure.

The crucible of personal choice. Here we explore what happens when we make decisions and choices that end up going terribly wrong, and we must confront the reality that our own moral choices make real and enduring impacts.

Throughout the book, I demonstrate how these seven crucibles relate to biblical principles that can inform and guide us. I also describe spiritual practices that not only sustain and guide us, but invite God to shape us into the person and leader he wants us to be. And I focus attention on the power and role of seeking meaning throughout every crucible experience. Each chapter ends with a reflection section. Taking the time to journal through the questions or discuss them with a mentor or group will deepen your understanding of how these crucibles are at play in your own life.

ENCOURAGEMENT TO ENDURE

If we want to invest our energy in purposes that outlive us, we must learn how to let God shape us in the midst of our crucibles. We choose whether we collapse under the weight of our struggles and calamities or rise to the challenges before us with God's help. Crucibles bring suffering but they also offer transformative opportunities that shape our character and help us become the best version of ourselves. As we respond, we can fulfill God's greatest purposes for our life.

In the pages that follow, I share my experiences and the lessons I learned with each crucible to encourage and inspire you to persevere in the midst of your own challenges. I believe you'll discover, as I did, a deep and abiding confidence in the goodness and grace of God. I pray you'll find strength to keep going and come to see crucibles not as barriers to God but as divine passageways that deepen your relationship with him and strengthen your character. In the process, I hope you discover a framework of meaning that inspires and guides you.

FOR REFLECTION

Philosopher Friedrich Nietzsche famously observed, "He who has a *why* to live can bear with almost any *how*."[2] The why question often determines how we understand pivotal moments in both life and leadership. Wrestling meaning out of crucibles requires cultivating internal conversations that increase self-awareness and enable us to self-correct when necessary. We can begin those conversations in the midst of a crucible by answering three soul-shaping questions:

Do I accurately see and understand what's happening to me? As we reflect on this question, we begin to recognize and identify the pivotal experiences of our life that have shaped us.

What is happening inside of me? Individuals, education, and work have influenced us, as have our family of origin and the family we develop. We draw on our memory, imagination, and will as we process these experiences, elevating some, diminishing others, and recognizing patterns and purposes that emerge over time.

What is happening because of me? As we consider the convictions arising from our experiences and reflect on our actions and accomplishments, we begin to understand the contribution we're making personally and professionally.

These questions help us think deeply about the crucibles challenging us and help us better respond to our trials, develop our character and our leadership, and grow closer to God throughout the process. Keep them in mind as you read about each of the seven crucibles.

1

THE CRUCIBLE OF MISSED MEANING

*But blessed are your eyes, for they see,
and your ears, for they hear [and understand].*

JESUS, MATTHEW 13:16

We had the experience, but we missed the meaning.

T. S. ELIOT, *FOUR QUARTETS*

SHORTLY AFTER BECOMING president of Westmont College in 2007, I met Mary Docter and Laura Montgomery, two veteran professors who developed the "cycle of global learning," a framework and philosophy for our study-abroad programs. The cycle of global learning can counteract T. S. Eliot's famous observation, "We had the experience, but we missed the meaning." This three-semester process begins with a pre-trip seminar that orients students to traveling internationally and understanding cultures different from their own. During the second semester, professors accompany students on their journey to help them interpret their experiences. The semester after the trip, students take a reentry seminar to bring the learning home.

In contrast, *the crucible of missed meaning* refers to the failure to perceive reality accurately. Misperception can lead to responses that miss the mark and fail to provide a successful strategy or solution. What we thought would work doesn't. Those we strive to lead become frustrated. Even though our idea looked great, it's impossible to implement in reality and causes a loss of confidence across the organization. How then do we learn to see and perceive, hear and understand?

In Matthew 13, Jesus says we'll always be seeing but never perceiving, always hearing, but never understanding. What applied in Jesus' day continues to be true today. We can be unwilling to truly see our current situation and its context accurately. How can we learn to look with the eyes of understanding and anticipate what's coming next? And once we see, or perceive, how do we make an appropriate and timely response?

Jesus taught in parables to help us make a gestalt shift and capture a deeper meaning and reality than we first perceived. Parables often reveal a central spiritual truth that brings insight into our human condition. This indirect approach penetrates our natural defenses that resist God. The Greek words for *seeing* and *perceiving* include both seeing with the eye and perceiving with the mind. Jesus encourages us to develop the capacity to look at a situation and perceive the deeper realities at play through our observation and experience.

In similar fashion, our contemporary context helps us recognize the ongoing challenge of perceiving reality accurately. Iris Murdoch writes poignantly about the nature of the spiritual life being a perpetual quest to perceive things as they really are, not as we wish they were.[1] She also notes that once we perceive reality accurately, we need to act correctly and appropriately. But how can we be sure that we're perceiving reality accurately and making an appropriate response? The answer lies in part in developing our capacity for perceptual insight.

When training a new leader or addressing a mistake, we often tend to focus on the presenting problem rather than the real problem.

When we get drawn into a situation, we may believe we've understood it adequately and created an appropriate response to get back on track. But in so many cases, we fail to stay emotionally connected and don't completely understand the problem. The remedy is to stay engaged but sufficiently differentiated, so that we can make course corrections as we refine our perception and gain wider understanding.

FOCUSED ATTENTION LEADS TO WIDER UNDERSTANDING

Effective leadership is built on focused attention, the ability to communicate, and the capacity to see how discrete particulars fit into a larger whole. In 2016, Charles Duhigg released his award-winning book *Smarter Faster Better*.[2] The volume presents a wide array of information in eight highly appealing, tightly written chapters, including one on focus. This chapter deals with the difference between the mass of people who see only discrete particulars and the exceptional but limited few who can weave these discrete particulars into a meaningful whole.

In one tragic example, he tells the sad and demoralizing story of an Air France jet that crashed due to "cognitive tunneling," the tendency of our brain to become overly focused on what's directly in front of us. This phenomenon causes all kinds of accidents, because we lose our ability to balance the need to focus on specific stimuli while simultaneously keeping a wider frame of reference that leads to good judgment.

To prevent cognitive tunneling, we need to learn how to create mental models that allow us to assimilate new information rapidly regardless of our circumstances. To illustrate the difference, Duhigg tells the riveting story of Darlene, a neonatal nurse with the unusual ability to spot a baby in distress before monitors signaled a problem. Her remarkable capacity resulted from a combination of technical competence, intuition, and expertise gained from thousands of hours of focused attention and practiced experience, which all contributed to sound medical judgment and a willingness to act. She could see and anticipate what was going to happen even before the sophisticated monitors and medical equipment sounded an alarm.

CULTURE AS A DIVINE PASSAGEWAY

How do we learn to see, perceive, and act in this way? One great example is found in the book of Acts. Acts 10 and 11 demonstrate how Peter learned to look with new eyes and see the work of God differently. Although culturally and religiously Jewish, Peter became the foundation of faith emblematic of the early church. His proximity to Jesus allowed him to reorient his perception, which brought understanding and growth to the first Christians. Known initially as an impulsive disciple given to defiant outbursts, Peter matured after years of discipline and devotion to Christ and steadfastly embodied God's love, goodness, and grace.

The incredible story begins in Acts 10 with Cornelius—a Roman centurion and a God-fearing, devout man, "generous to those in need and given to regular prayer." An angel tells him to send for Peter. Meanwhile, Peter has a vision in which God tells him to kill and eat animals devout Jews considered unclean. Peter struggles to make sense of his dream because his plausibility structure limits his understanding. He not only blunders initially; he repeats himself and errs a second time. He struggles like so many of us because his cultural perception of life prevents him from embracing multiple ways to see and respond to God.

When the three men arrive from Caesarea and ask him to visit Cornelius, Peter realizes their information is directly related to the meaning of his dream, and he begins to perceive God's greater purposes. Neither Cornelius nor Peter have yet fully understood the purposes of God in the world. As their encounter unfolds, Peter stumbles beyond the narrow understanding of his provincial worldview.

He struggles like so many of us because his cultural perception of life prevents him from embracing multiple ways to see and respond to God.

Peter eventually discerns that cultures serve not as barriers to human understanding but as divine passageways to God. So often culture leads us to focus on our differences, but God uses cultural differences between Peter and Cornelius to engineer a pivotal breakthrough to a higher level of understanding.

A few chapters later, in Acts 15, Peter draws on his new perception at the Jerusalem Council. In this later encounter, the early church gathers its luminaries to determine what requirements to place on new Gentile converts. The exchange begins with Peter recounting his own journey to perceptual insight in a brilliant, concise, and compelling message: what God has done for us, he has also done for the Gentiles. Peter has witnessed this new reality. His experience and conceptual understanding help him recognize how God works in the world. He embodies the reality that new perceptions lead to better communities, more sophisticated understanding, and greater empathy and awareness on both a local and global scale. By Acts 15, his thinking and perceiving have matured, and he becomes the spokesperson for the transformational shift in how the early church will accept non-Jewish converts, thereby transforming Christianity into a global movement.

MOVING BEYOND OUR BIASES TO PERCEIVE THE WHOLE

Since global Christianity is so obviously a result of a growth mindset, what holds us back? What makes us prefer one type of people over another? The answer lies in the important work that is being done to understand implicit bias.

Implicit bias refers to the universal condition of preferring people who look like us, think like us, live like us. We develop a bias for things we know and like, which often causes us to misread and misunderstand our circumstances. Leaders can be especially prone to this condition.

In 2014, Pope Francis invited a group I was a part of to travel to the Vatican as a contingent of Protestant and Orthodox Christians working in various spheres of society. My long career and experience in faith-based higher education led to my inclusion. Eventually, I received an appointment to the Vatican Foundation for the Family, a council on which I still serve.

I found the brevity and clarity of the invitation from Pope Francis the most interesting aspect of this opportunity: "We've been fighting for five hundred years. Can we try to find common cause together by focusing on our mutual commitment to the life and ministry of Jesus?" In this pithy request, Pope Francis distilled the violent and pitched opposition that had marked so much of church history in the Western world. He asked us to focus not on our differences but on what we held in common. The invitation encouraged us to move beyond so many of the parochial religious habits we practice to gain a transformed vision of God's work in the world.

Our visit coincided with a worldwide conference of the Catholic Charismatic Renewal, a movement that started in 1967 at Duquesne University in Pittsburgh. Gathered in Rome's Olympic Stadium, these believers represented roughly 135 million of the 1.2 billion Catholic Christians around the world. Many eye-opening, perspective-shifting experiences occurred every day during the time of gathered worship as we sang praise choruses familiar to us but echoing throughout the stadium in a foreign tongue in the heart of Catholicism.

I saw in that moment how experience can be a great teacher, but only if we adequately interpret it and accurately understand it. I enlarged my perspective by taking the discrete experiences I was having and seeing them whole, as so many of us can learn to do. In the midst of the crucible of missed meaning, we need to seek ever-deeper levels of understanding.

In *The Structure of Scientific Revolutions*, Thomas Kuhn coins the phrase "plausibility structures," or mental models, to describe how we understand the world and our place in it.[3] These worldviews often become shorthand ways we see and perceive others. As we weave our discrete experiences into meaningful wholes and develop an understanding of the world, we can form biases that distort our view of reality. When our perceptions fail to fit comfortably within our current structure of meaning, we either expand our mental model to gain deeper insight, or our view of the world ceases to make sense of our lived experience.

CULTIVATING HUMILITY, CURIOSITY, AND UNDERSTANDING

In Acts, Peter teaches us that we need a disposition of humility that opens us to learning. Developing such a teachable spirit is the hallmark of an *apprentice*, someone who actively cultivates humility, curiosity, and learning to better understand.[4]

A beautiful picture of developing these characteristics appears in a brief exchange between characters played by Sally Field and John Malkovich in the movie *Places in the Heart*.[5] Set during the Great Depression, the film depicts Edna Spalding, a widow played by Field, trying to keep her farm after the untimely, accidental killing of her husband, the local sheriff. To help make ends meet, Edna has rented a room to Mr. Will, a blind man played by Malkovich. Mr. Will asks Edna questions, such as: What color is your hair? What color are your eyes? Through this exchange, Mr. Will gives us a deeper, more visual recognition of Edna. Here's the brief dialogue:

Mr. Will: Mrs. Spalding, can I ask you a question?

Edna: Yes.

Mr. Will: What do you look like?

Edna: I have long hair and I tie it up at the back. And I have
            brown eyes. I always wanted to have blue eyes like my
            mama but Margaret got those. And, my teeth stick out
            a little out front. Because I sucked my thumb for a long
            time when I was a little girl. No real beauty. I'm all right.

Mr. Will: Thank you.

Humble curiosity drives Mr. Will's questions, and he helps us see and understand Edna's deeper qualities and subtle beauty. In the same way, the blind man also allows us to recognize the strength and reliability of Moze Hadner, a Black field hand played by Danny Glover; the identity of the violent men cloaked in ominous KKK robes through the sound of their voices; and even the role religion plays in daily life. Mr. Will teaches us to look beyond the surface of people and situations with wider interest and deeper understanding, a key to navigating the crucible of missed meaning.

The movie ends with a surreal worship service that includes a celebration of Communion foreshadowing an eternity in heaven. Field's husband reappears, passing the Communion tray to the young teenager who accidentally shot him. This magical realism, reminiscent of Gabriel García Márquez's *One Hundred Years of Solitude*, helps us recognize the presence of God's kingdom everywhere and the constant co-mingling of the temporal and eternal in our everyday life. It invites us to perceive human reality in a new way. We're all children of God and belong to the kingdom of God, eternally present in temporal time. This refined perception helps us understand that we humans erect our barriers to understanding, not God.

LEARNING TO "READ THE AIR"

These reflections, both on the realities of the world and on our life with God, teach us a great deal about the challenges of leadership. So often we get mired in the minutiae of running an organization that we lose our perspective. We hesitate to step back and see how the discrete particulars fit into a meaningful whole. But one of the great disciplines of leadership is learning how to pierce the veil of presenting problems to see the real issues.

Over time, I've come to recognize the importance of framing our realities accurately because that plays a fundamental role in what we think we should do. I consistently feel drawn to third-way solutions, going beyond either-or to find a third way to solve problems we haven't yet considered. We must stoke our curiosity and look for alternatives to our current ways of thinking and seeing.

In 1992, my wife, Pam, and I traveled to Wuhan, China, to help midlevel professors at Wuhan University of Technology gain proficiency in spoken English. Most of our students already read and wrote the language, but hearing and recognizing English presents a different and more complex challenge. Watching our students suddenly begin to hear and understand spoken English fascinated and rewarded us. This achievement arose from developing the competency of focused attention and learning the ability to see the word as part of a larger whole—in this case through the structure of sentences and paragraphs.

Leaders face similar challenges in terms of recognizing when we're understanding and being understood and when we aren't. Erin Meyer teaches us to "read the air."[6] This is the learned capacity to perceive both the discrete particulars represented by individual words and the greater meaning represented by understanding the meaning of each word in a larger context.

In *The Culture Map*, Meyer articulates her compelling overview of eight primary categories by which we map cultural understanding: communicating, evaluating, leading, deciding, trusting, disagreeing, scheduling, and persuading.[7] In each case, she provides a spectrum of perspectives that help us gain insight so our crosscultural communication can function effectively.

For example, she identifies polar opposites in communication as "low context" and "high context." Low-context languages include American and British English, which tend to communicate directly and specifically. High-context languages like Japanese rely not only on words but on the context for the communication. She encourages us to learn how to read the air in order to understand the cultural signals of non-verbal communication.

Daniel Kahneman's *Thinking, Fast and Slow*, based on his Nobel Prize–winning work, beautifully articulates a complementary insight.[8] In this groundbreaking classic, he distills a number of relevant principles and insights, including his cautionary acronym WYSIATI, "What you see is all there is." This acronym reflects the human tendency to exaggerate our grasp of situations and circumstances when we actually lack adequate understanding.[9] As Kahneman notes, this disposition leads to arrogance, and our self-importance causes us to miss the way that so many discrete particulars of life only make sense when placed together into meaningful wholes. Our capacity for pattern recognition serves as a bridge to deeper understanding.

Kahneman and his late friend and co-collaborator, Amos Tversky, articulate so many groundbreaking discoveries in this book: confirmation bias, priming effect, the reflexive response of regret, the tendency to ignore data we can't see, the widely misleading tendency to weigh evidence inappropriately, and much more. They even reveal the real motivator of economic behavior as loss avoidance—not profit-maximization, as the Chicago school and others have argued. Their work demonstrates how often what we believe merely results from the way our mind creates mental maps that promote shortcuts in decision-making. Rarely accurate, these shortcuts can be highly misleading and, in some instances, catastrophic.

BUILDING MENTAL MODELS

How then do we learn how to slow down, look with curiosity, and see with understanding? We need to build mental models, or structures of meaning, that help us make sense of life as we experience it. Ten years ago I wrote *The Shaping of an Effective Leader*, which reflected my thinking during the previous twenty years, including time spent studying with management consultant Peter Drucker and consolidating my thoughts into an eight-tier pyramid.[10] This structure incorporated the wisdom of key mentors, the keen insight of a variety of educational influences, and the practical wisdom of professional experiences, all of which had influenced my personal and professional development as a leader.

Five years ago, I was asked to develop an eighteen-minute TED talk on leadership. As I reworked my pyramid, I realized I could consolidate my thinking into a Venn diagram with three overlapping circles highlighting the intersection of intelligence (born of education and guided experience), empathy (born of moral and emotional intelligence), and creativity (born of innovation and strategic risk-taking). The dynamic intersection of these three categories forms the heart of strategic effectiveness.

Figure 1.1. The heart of strategic effectiveness

Most recently, I've refined my thinking further into these seven crucibles that shape us. More crucibles exist, but I consider these seven to be the dominant archetypes that inform our common experience. *Missed meaning* and *awakened moral conscience* are embedded with intelligence and require education and guided experience to respond well. *Enduring challenge* and *social conflict* are embedded in creativity and require innovation and strategic risk-taking to endure. *Human treachery* and *human suffering* are embedded in empathy and inform the foundational experiences that lead to our growth in moral and emotional intelligence. At the heart of strategic effectiveness are the multiple personal choices that determine our life destiny.

Together, these mental models, or frameworks of meaning, provide the architecture I need both to understand and communicate how I approach leadership and seek to fulfill my responsibilities. This structure has helped me develop a disposition of daily prayer and meditation, both for centering my life in God and for gaining deeper self-awareness and self-understanding. Specifically, I pray through my known schedule for the day, recognizing that during the school year, the day rarely begins and ends as I expect. Through the process of spiritual centering, I see and receive input that strengthens my perceptions and insight so I can self-correct when necessary.

I've developed a rich appreciation for the roles and responsibilities of various sectors of our organization and how much we can do when we focus on our core work—and how much can be destroyed when we get out of our appropriate lane. Defining our role is so important and requires trust among team members. We need to be aware of the possibility of saboteurs and charlatans.

Clarity of purpose helps us build sound strategies, which provide the confidence to engage in successful execution. It guides the hiring and retention of top people who are competent and driven to succeed. Our commitment to create a culture of integrity, care, and respect plays a crucial role in how we act—and we fully recognize this goal as aspirational and requiring continuous improvement.

Ultimately, we have to be committed to purposes greater than ourselves and be driven by a vision that exceeds inconvenience. We seldom see the entire vision clearly, and we often only realize it over time. We can find joy in encountering the crucible of missed meaning because it refines our character and helps us develop a greater capacity to engage the opportunities before us, instead of suffering indifference or paralysis, which keep us from a greater good.

BIBLICAL INSIGHT FROM PAUL AND THE ATHENIANS

Years ago, Don Richardson, a famous missiologist, wrote *Peace Child*.[11] This book seeks to demonstrate that every culture possesses a story of redemption that Christians can reference when explaining Christ's work. Initially a groundbreaking idea, the concept has since faced challenges. But the seed of insight it planted helped Christians see culture as an asset rather than a liability in communicating Christ's story to the world.

Even before *Peace Child*, philosophers of religion identified three types of religious worldviews: exclusive, inclusive, and pluralist. The exclusive worldview sees few if any overlapping ideas among various religions. The inclusive worldview believes all religions find their greatest expression in Christianity. Pluralists consider all religions to be about the same. I'm an inclusivist and believe all religious worldviews can be understood within the Christian worldview.

Acts 17:16-32 provides a beautiful example of how cultures serve as divine passageways to the gospel rather than barriers to belief in God. They help us understand how God works in the world. While in Athens, a city rife with idols, the apostle Paul refrains from railing against paganism. Instead, he appeals to their obvious religious devotion, demonstrating in five important ways how we can build bridges of insight and understanding between Christianity and all other religious and philosophical worldviews.

First, Paul begins by showing respect for worldviews other than his own by acknowledging their religious outlook. "People of Athens!" he begins, "I see that in every way you are very religious. For as I walked around and looked carefully at your objects of worship, I even found an altar with this inscription: TO AN UNKNOWN GOD" (Acts 17:22-23 NIV).

Second, he goes on to explain how their partial awareness can lead to understanding the full nature of God. Paul explains God's true nature when he declares, "The God who made the world and everything in it is the Lord of heaven and earth and does not live in temples built by human hands. And he is not served by human hands, as if he needed anything. Rather, he himself gives everyone life and breath and everything else" (Acts 17:24-25 NIV).

As Paul continues, he then reveals every religious longing as a remnant of the God-shaped vacuum God created in us. Saint Augustine wrote, "Our hearts are restless until they find their rest in you, O God."[12] In verses 26 and 27, Paul articulates the purposes of Christ and notes that God has given us a desire to see and find him. A God-shaped instinct and desire motivates our ultimate search for meaning and purpose.

Paul appeals to them by using their own literature to illustrate his fourth point. He tells his listeners that their own literature captures their longing for God: "As some of your own poets have said, 'We are his offspring'" (Acts 17:28 NIV). Paul notes how their tradition dovetails beautifully with the truth about God. This insight demonstrates how we eventually awaken to our need for Christ and illustrates how every religious quest prompts us to get underway. Eventually, we need guidance and direction to find ultimate satisfaction.

He finally clarifies a fifth way that their religious practices lead them to a mistaken understanding of God's nature. Paul says to the Athenians, "Therefore since we are God's offspring, we should not think that the divine being is like gold or silver or stone—an image made by human design and skill" (Acts 17:29 NIV). He elevates both

God and his listeners by identifying them as the offspring of the ruler of the universe who has provided the ultimate satisfaction for human longing through the person and work of Jesus Christ.

Paul's encounter with the Athenians ends with an honest appraisal of how people receive the gospel: some believe, some scoff, and some have more questions (Acts 17:32-34). Every encounter with God generates one of these three responses, often within the same group of listeners.

This passage offers a key insight into the crucible of missed understanding. We often believe that everyone who hears the gospel automatically believes. But the actual reality is just the opposite. Every individual comes to believe on a timetable known only to God; therefore, our limited energy and focus should be on those who awaken to faith and our deeper life with God and respond in repentance or curiosity. The time has not yet come for those who scoff, and we might never be the appropriate vessel.

FOR REFLECTION

1. Identify a time you've been involved in crosscultural communication. How was culture a barrier, and how was it a bridge to deeper insight and understanding?

2. When you encounter cultures and ideas different from your own, do you tend to shut them out (exclusivist), fully embrace them (pluralist), or look for ways they more fully contribute to and help build your deeper understanding of God (inclusivist)?

3. In what ways has your understanding of God grown and changed throughout your life as a result of travel or living and working in cultures different from your own?

4. What do people see of Christ when they encounter you?

2

THE CRUCIBLE OF ENDURING CHALLENGE

We rejoice in our sufferings, knowing that suffering produces endurance, and endurance produces character, and character produces hope.

ROMANS 5:3-4

[My] success consists of going from one failure to the next without loss of enthusiasm.

SIR WINSTON CHURCHILL

NO OTHER CRUCIBLE does more to develop personal wisdom than the *crucible of enduring challenge*. Although we wish our life and our leadership responsibilities were consistent from day to day, they rarely are. Though every leader faces enormous challenges that require a response, it's still difficult to anticipate the severity of unfolding events and the length of time it will take to resolve them. Each situation demands a vision that exceeds inconvenience and a commitment to strategies and tactics that help us persevere. Let me begin by suggesting twelve enduring lessons I've learned along the way that can guide you on your own leadership journey.

- Enjoy today; tomorrow has enough worries of its own.

- Never open a two-front war if you can help it.

- Don't overreact to overreactions.

- Don't say everything you think (I've never gotten in trouble for things I thought but didn't say).

- Stay emotionally present even when you don't feel like it.

- I've never had an opportunity expand without a potential problem expanding with it.

- Be disciplined with what you share and with whom you share it.

- Avoid no-win arguments; it's like wrestling with a pig. You both get dirty, and the pig loves it.

- Cultivate a results-oriented mindset with attention to doing the right activities.

- Cultivate an aspiring edge that stimulates hope and renewal.

- Maintain a commitment to open communication and conflict resolution.

- Always work to outlast the opposition except when you know it's the right time to leave for the right reason.

No special method or secret way can keep an organization on track. Regardless of the challenge, we must stay vigilant about the mission and purpose and not let all that happens to us and around us be a distraction. We wish we could find the secret formula, but everything we know suggests we just have to do the work.

When I was interviewing for the presidency at Westmont, the people who met with me asked how I would keep the college from wandering away from its mission. They asked the question with the unspoken assumption that colleges, like countries, intend to endure. I share this assumption, but I responded by answering that I could only guarantee that I'd show up every single day prepared to do the work to stay on course. I explained that I've seen many boards and administrations that believe putting leadership on autopilot will ensure everything naturally stays on course; the reality is just the opposite. Unless you stay vigilant, organizations—like individuals—always wander off. How, then, do we cultivate the resilience and perseverance to stay the course?

Scripture teaches that these qualities grow out of our life with God, and it emphasizes the importance of persevering in the face of obstacles and setbacks. In truth, anything worth doing will take time, effort, and human ingenuity. As others have noted, all good plans eventually degenerate into hard work. Through persevering, we not only develop our responses and plans, but we learn how to adjust to changing circumstances to make the contribution God put us on earth to make. Our character develops as we become the best expression of ourselves. At some point, we realize we're committing our life to purposes that will outlive us.

Recently, cognitive and behavioral psychologists identified the benefits of perseverance in the face of challenge, and resilience in response to setbacks. Although earlier scholars believed we possessed a certain setpoint or threshold of resilience, new research demonstrates that every one of us can grow in our capacity to endure.[1] In other words, two people can encounter the same situation and react very differently due to the individual experience of learning how to bounce back from a crisis.

As an individual or organization perseveres, they build confidence by learning to develop a capacity to recover. This assurance then comes into play when new experiences of adversity and challenge materialize. History is dotted with leaders who rose to the challenge to meet their circumstances. Winston Churchill, one of the most striking examples, experienced equal parts triumph, tragedy, heroism, and controversy throughout his life and career.[2]

WINSTON CHURCHILL'S EXTRAORDINARY PERSEVERANCE

Churchill famously said, "When you're going through hell, keep going!" He remains one of history's most significant figures, in part because of all he overcame. My lifelong interest in Churchill stems from growing up in Eugene, Oregon, and attending Winston Churchill High School. During my time there, I studied with a wonderful English teacher who routinely asked us to memorize and recite Churchill's great quotes and barbed quips. I continue to reflect on his many heroic triumphs, well-known catastrophes, remarkable capacity for overcoming, tireless drive, and legendary leadership during and following World War II. I especially appreciate his amazing confidence that he rose to power for a particular reason that served purposes greater than himself.[3]

Despite his controversial position on some matters, including his perspective on the British Empire itself, writers and scholars continue to ponder in thousands of pages of print what made Churchill unique, legendary, and effective. In fact, it is quite striking to note that of the secondary works on Churchill that I consulted, almost all of them have been published in the last eight to ten years, illustrating his continuing appeal even as we move deeper into the twenty-first century. He demonstrated a persevering spirit nearly unmatched in political history. Some focus on his challenging upbringing: his father disparaged him, and his mother loved but neglected him. Others highlight his keen sense of humor. Still others focus on his unique combination of personal hardship and professional success that gave him the confidence to continue in the face of catastrophe.[4]

In books by and about Churchill, distinct themes emerge that offer enduring lessons for all leaders. First, he possessed a unique capacity to hold strong convictions but remain flexible if new situations led him to respond differently than originally thought or planned. As his capture, imprisonment, and eventual escape during the Boer War demonstrated, he was amazingly innovative when he had to be. His reservoir of restlessness and bias for action helped him push through setbacks to find new solutions.[5]

Legendary for his curiosity, he wondered first and foremost about the nature and reach of the British Empire. As an adult, he requested specific assignments that took him to the Far East and South Africa, both to stoke his sense of adventure and to contribute to his Anglocentric worldview.[6] After the debacle of the Gallipoli campaign in 1915, Churchill volunteered for army duty on the frontlines in Belgium. During World War II, he traveled more than any other world leader to evaluate troop movements, negotiate treaties, and extract promises and resources that helped Britain fight the war.[7]

Churchill was a tactile learner deeply influenced by his surroundings. Spatial relocation often triggered his creativity. He teaches us the importance of moving about to stimulate fresh ideas.

Like his travel, his curiosity also led him to explore with an unmatched intensity and energy every topic that intrigued him.[8] His insatiable need to know helped him build a storehouse of ideas and innovations that informed his strategic decision-making even under the most severe, pressure-packed circumstances. What a great lesson for leaders: spend time filling your mind with all manner of information, recognizing that your creative problem-solving will benefit in the future from your curiosity and learning today.

The attitude we carry into hardship also matters. Churchill's amazing capacity to stay optimistic despite his circumstances is remarkable. He also never seems to have lost his sense of humor. His resilience and resourcefulness in the face of monumental challenges produced some of the most notable exchanges ever recorded,[9] including his legendary and memorable rejoinders to Lady Asquith. Even his multiple encounters with lesser-known opponents prove illuminating. An angry voter once confronted him and exclaimed, "Vote for you? Why I'd rather vote for the devil!" To which Churchill responded, "I understand, but in case your friend is not running, may I count on your support?"[10] What a wonderful, disarming way to meet the opposition!

Too often, political figures use public arenas to settle private scores. The public forgets what caused the offense, and only the baited response endures—almost always with a negative aftertaste. It's good to remind leaders in all arenas of the necessity to absorb personal criticism without retaliating.[11]

Churchill avoided public scandal tied to personal misconduct, which is striking in our modern era. He endured political debacles and failed strategies, but no one ever attacked his personal integrity. Many of his musings about private matters focused on one of his family members or close friends. Although surrounded by vice, he didn't seem drawn to it.

His marriage to Clementine grounded Churchill's own life, and he found energy and joy in it.[12] None of the well-documented difficulties in the relationship gave rise to the infidelities so often associated with acclaimed political leaders. His marriage provided the stable personal life almost always necessary for great leadership.[13] Such constancy allows leaders to direct their energy and intellect toward greater purposes that, in turn, allow them to make enduring contributions to society and the public good. When unhindered by dark clouds on the home front, leaders can marshal the necessary resources, both personal and social, to make sound judgments and craft effective and enduring strategies.

Consider the supporting evidence documented in the Harvard Study of Adult Development, an eighty-five-year longitudinal project that underscores the importance of a stable personal life. In 1938, a research team began studying 268 Harvard sophomore men. The initial group included a young President John F. Kennedy. One of the most interesting findings concludes that the quality of our relationships and our happiness with them exerts a powerful influence on our health. More than money or fame, close relationships keep people happy. This bliss helps delay physical, mental, and emotional decline. For leaders, it also provides the source of joy and contentment that makes personal and professional sacrifices meaningful.[14]

Ultimately, Churchill exuded a personal and public love and interest in other people—and most notably, an enduring love and interest in his country and its enlightened principles of democratic governance and self-rule. These passions propelled him across a sea of challenge with the bright light of his persevering spirit always guiding him.[15] The key principle: always give your life energies to purposes that will outlive you.

AN EARLIER EXAMPLE: FREDERICK DOUGLASS

During the global pandemic, we brought Nancy Koehn, a Harvard business historian and scholar, to campus via Zoom. In preparation for her visit, we read her award-winning work *Forged in Crisis*. Her book includes an important treatment of Frederick Douglass, a man emancipated from slavery who contributed so much to the abolishment of slavery in our country. Douglass's remarkable biography illustrates great principles of leadership. Having broken free from the shackles of slavery, he became a leading thinker, writer, and public intellectual for abolition.

Koehn's fascinating treatment helps us see Douglass's unique leadership gifts, including the remarkable observational skills so essential for leadership.[16] Douglass endured enormous setback and challenge. Drawn to like-minded abolitionists who defended him, he also endured the hatred and animosity of opponents who sought not only to inhibit his success as a champion of the abolitionist cause but also to destroy him personally. Over time, he developed an idealistic pragmatism that kept lofty ideals in front of him while developing strategies and tactics on the ground that would work.

Douglass recognized that he had to work within the context of his situation, leveraging the country's core founding documents to move forward, a practical reality that foreshadowed one of Martin Luther King Jr.'s unique strategies and insights. As he hungered for a strategic advantage, Douglass pursued a relationship with President Lincoln and became an important talking partner as Lincoln grew in his commitment to ending slavery. Douglass helps us see that birthright and upbringing never determine our destiny. A purpose in life and a vision that exceeds the inconvenience are key drivers of social change and the role our personal contribution can play in making it.

Douglass also recognized where he could make his greatest contribution. Working with a keen sense of human nature, he knew when to negotiate his way out of situations and when to hold his ground. This is critical in all facets of leadership.

Eventually, Douglass recognized he could best use his time and talent by demonstrating how far a person could develop when given the freedom and resources to cultivate their gifts and abilities. We can't just act. We have to weigh the impact of our contribution and consider both individually and corporately how we can make the widest, most profound impact possible.

Ultimately, when we act out of a sense of moral purpose, we understand it's the right thing to do. We never know if it will turn out to be successful or even make a lasting contribution; we simply choose a path and move in a certain direction because our conscience allows no other choice.

BUILDING MENTAL MAPS THAT HELP US ENDURE

Churchill and Douglass both demonstrate that leading under duress is exhausting, but it's almost always the reality we face. We're conditioned by our education to believe that life is predictable and circumstances on the ground are reasonable and exactly what we believe them to be. But the reality is often just the opposite. Circumstances change and fortunes shift, and we have to develop the instincts and the energy to change with them. This doesn't mean we jettison the past. Instead, the time-bound realities and challenges we face help us learn how to stay emotionally present, so we can understand and differentiate the timeless principles that define our purpose and reason for being. This is *why* we lead. Henry Kissinger's latest book helps us understand *how*.

Never a head of state himself, Kissinger wrote his latest book, *Leadership*, about six world leaders he knew and worked with directly and the principles that influenced and ultimately guided them. In particular, he considers the significant seasons of trial and setback they confronted and how their response affected their leadership and shaped their enduring contribution. In 2013, I had the privilege of hosting Kissinger at Westmont when he spoke at our Mosher Center for Moral and Ethical Leadership lecture series, an annual event that elevates the importance of moral and ethical leadership in all dimensions and areas of life. Despite the passage of time and his advancing age, his presence was still mildly controversial.

Nevertheless I was determined to be a gracious host, and as we traveled from the airport to our Westmont gathering, I expressed appreciation for his long career, including his significant body of written work. As we neared campus, I asked him what, if anything, seemed new to him. To my distinct surprise, he mentioned that he had become more mindful of the unique benefits of a devout religious upbringing, whether it be Jewish, Christian, or otherwise. What an interesting insight.

In *Leadership*, Kissinger identifies qualities necessary for extraordinary leadership, including the tireless drive to achieve enduring results. He amplifies his main points somewhat surprisingly by focusing on the important combination of character and circumstance. Having been at the center of power and controversy, Kissinger shows how leadership becomes especially important during times of crisis, rapid change, or jarring economic and political dislocation.

The responsibility of leadership includes expanding existing institutions to mark progress and preserve positive new developments and change.[17] A corollary duty: do no harm. Elevating the timeless over the time-bound in our organizations and through our opportunities requires insight and awareness.

It's critical for a leader to cultivate an aspirational edge that's never satisfied. History demonstrates that specific societies and entire civilizations stall out when they lose their aspiring edge. The same is true of individuals.

Another essential component to leadership is a robust formal education that makes lifelong learning possible, both in the immediate and in the long-term. This priority highlights the importance of learning as we develop our competence and character, and preparing for a yet undefined future before making an overt contribution. A vigorous education can also give us a foundation for a meaningful life.

Intellectual curiosity is a must. It cultivates capacities and carries us beyond our current circumstances in both expansive and instructive ways. This knowledge helps form mental models that guide our perspective and ultimately contributes to the shape of our proposed solutions.

Religious and moral values are essential. They provide guidance and structure our life. They cultivate the courage to act in the face of incomplete information. One of the most important lessons I've learned is the importance of being willing to engage in creative risk-taking that inevitably produces some mistakes. But this also provides an incredible opportunity to learn from strategies and actions that initially failed as we develop a greater capacity to craft strategies and actions that ultimately succeed. Consider a few of Kissinger's examples.

Konrad Adenauer. He rose to power immediately after World War II as the first chancellor of Germany following Adolf Hitler. His Catholic upbringing deeply grounded and guided him, helping Adenauer balance integrity of purpose with genuine goodwill. Believing that "politics is pragmatic action for the sake of moral good," he acted on his political and religious values.[18]

Richard Nixon. A controversial figure, Nixon brought vast political experience and know-how to the presidency, but the political and cultural atmosphere had changed completely since he left the public stage eight years earlier. Despite his public persona and conservative legacy, Nixon worked tirelessly to find solutions to social problems that fit the nation's cultural values. Although a polarizing figure himself, he helped resolve some of the deeper social conflicts percolating just beneath the surface of American society. Beyond his moral lapses, his most besetting sin as a leader involved his tendency to settle petty scores with lesser opponents.[19]

Lee Kuan Yew. As the founding prime minister of Singapore, Lee deeply understood the vulnerability of his infant country, but he refused to focus on its limitations. His ingenuity and discipline carved a cultural identity of excellence that still guides Singapore today. He demonstrates what one person can achieve when they set a tone and a direction that honors the past, faithfully manages the present, and strategically maps the future. His focus helped establish the principles of prosperity and the importance of ethical guidelines that allow people at all levels of society to flourish.[20]

Margaret Thatcher. Thatcher was the first female prime minister of Great Britain and the one who served the longest in the twentieth century (1979 to 1990); she was a highly principled, deeply religious person. As she faced great challenges both within her own party and throughout her political career, she made significant strides forward while learning how to bounce back from legendary defeats. Firmly held principles guided her leadership: a strong and enduring commitment to the sovereignty of nations, a belief in the fundamental value of every human, a commitment to the importance of the rule of law, and faith in the free-market economic system with its limited government and its ability to promote human flourishing.

Occasionally tone deaf to matters of public sentiment, Thatcher eventually lost her position during significant reversals in 1990. Her deeply held convictions and beliefs helped her demonstrate the importance of being consistent, dependable, and predictable. She also led with dignity and grace. If not always effective, she inspired many and activated the cultural resources of a great country emerging from a period of stagnation and decline.[21]

WHY FAITH MATTERS

As Kissinger concludes, he echoes a theme I first heard from him in our car ride from the airport: the unique and fundamental importance of a religious upbringing. "A key factor common to each of the leaders [except Lee, whose guiding principles are clearly Confucian, and although not explicitly religious, Confucian principles are deeply philosophical and form a coherent philosophy of life] was a devout religious upbringing—Catholic for Adenauer and de Gaulle, Quaker for Nixon, Sunni Muslim for Sadat and Methodist for Thatcher."[22] He adds a lengthy quote from Alexis de Tocqueville's *Democracy in America,* to underscore his point: "The devout are accustomed to consider for a long succession of years an unmoving object toward which they constantly advance, and they learn by insensible progressions to repress a thousand little passing desires. . . . This explains why religious people have often accomplished such lasting things. In occupying themselves with the other world, they encountered the great secret of succeeding in this one."[23]

Churchill made a similar point about the demise of the Roman Empire and the enduring importance and persistence of the Christian faith:

> After the fall of Imperial Rome, the victorious barbarians were
> in their turn captivated and enthralled by the Gospel of Christ.
> Though no more successful in laying aside their sinful promptings
> than religious men and women are today, they had a common

theme and inspiration. There was a bond which linked all the races of Europe. . . . In this era, the Christian Church became the sole sanctuary of learning and knowledge. . . . Amid the turbulence and ignorance of the age of Roman decay, all the intellectual elements at first found refuge in the Church, and afterwards exercised mastery from it. Here was the school of politicians.[24]

THE POWER OF GRATITUDE

The emergence of neuroscience has helped us apply insights from brain science in understanding the complexity of perseverance and challenge, particularly in leadership and decision-making. This area of study explains the role certain behaviors and practices play over time in wiring and rewiring our brain. The expression of gratitude is one striking example. The habit of identifying specific experiences for which we're grateful fundamentally wires our brain in ways that help us persevere. Specific strategies demonstrate the importance of practicing personal discipline and emotional intelligence to help us make the right response, at the right time, for the right reason, in the right way. This allows us to develop the mental muscle to endure well.

The word *gratitude* comes from Latin and has a variety of meanings, including a sense of gratefulness for positive outcomes. It also recognizes the contributions of others and our responses to key events, which all contribute meaningful guideposts in life. In particular, researchers have determined that cultivating a spirit of gratefulness strengthens our perseverance because it bolsters other positive emotions, like joy and positivity, while counteracting negative emotions, such as envy, contempt, and anger, essential capacities in enduring well.[25]

As scholars continue to demonstrate the importance of viewing our circumstances as inherently good, they also recognize the need to develop a mindset that values perseverance.[26] Learning to look for the positives in every situation, learning to control what we can control—our attitude and our effort—and creating relational networks that provide support, encouragement, and appropriate perceptions of ourselves all help us endure. Gratitude bears measurable fruit.[27]

Leaders must realize that every organization, institution, or country faces great challenges and will drift without effective leadership. We can find an equilibrium that balances ambitions with abiding values by honoring the past and mapping the future. Often, we innovate within the box of history and future opportunity governed by context. These aspirations set the parameters within which every leader must respond to their own crucibles of enduring challenge.

BIBLICAL INSIGHT DEMONSTRATED IN FAITHFUL PERSEVERANCE

Three passages of Scripture guide our reflection and understanding.

Romans 5:3-5 teaches us the importance of resiliency, perseverance, and endurance: "We rejoice in our sufferings, knowing that suffering produces endurance, and endurance produces character, and character produces hope, and hope does not put us to shame, because God's love has been poured into our hearts through the Holy Spirit who has been given to us."

Suffering. Endurance. Character. Hope. God's love. Paul encourages us to stay true to our convictions and beliefs so we recognize in our own spirit the spirit of God, which is love. Our character is shaped through our experiences and our response to opportunities, setbacks, and challenges that test our convictions. Character gives rise to the general experience of hope and the specific realities in our life through which we experience the presence and love of God.

James 1:2-4 (NIV), a complementary passage, highlights the importance of perseverance in day-to-day challenges and in becoming the best expression of ourselves: "Consider it pure joy . . . whenever you face trials of many kinds, because you know that the testing of your faith produces perseverance. Let perseverance finish its work so that you may be mature and complete, not lacking anything." Perseverance conveys the sense of bearing up under huge challenges. Maturity results from a process. Coming to completion—*telos*, one of the most beautiful words in the New Testament—signifies how we achieve the full expression of who we are created to be in Christ Jesus. What we view as a setback and challenge God uses to bring us to the fullest understanding of his presence in our life and his love expressed through us.

Finally, how do we know when to broaden our convictions to accept new knowledge that helps us understand and embrace the wider purposes of God at work in the world? As we strive to persevere in faithfulness, we return to Acts 15:1-35 to see the role the Jerusalem Council played in adjudicating disputes among the first Christians. This early lesson communicates an enduring reality: everything that lasts needs a structure establishing meaning and guiding practice.

Luke reports in Acts 15 (NIV):

> Certain people came down from Judea to Antioch and were teaching the believers: "Unless you are circumcised, according to the custom taught by Moses, you cannot be saved." This brought Paul and Barnabas into sharp dispute and debate with them. . . . The apostles and elders met to consider this question. After much discussion, Peter got up and addressed them: "Brothers, you know that some time ago God made a choice among you that the Gentiles might hear from my lips the message of the gospel and believe. God, who knows the heart, showed that he accepted them by giving the Holy Spirit to them, just as he did to us. He did not discriminate between us and them. . . . It is my judgment, therefore, that we should not make it difficult for the Gentiles who are turning to God."

This passage illustrates how we can remain faithful to our experiences of God while producing effective responses to enduring challenges. By learning to welcome new converts into its communities of faith, the church has persevered through two thousand years of persecution and challenge. In Acts, the early Christians faced trials and tribulations requiring their ultimate sacrifice. Their endurance in the face of challenge created the institution of the church, which continues as God's enduring witness in the world. These early Christians embraced the dual realities of faithfulness to their own experiences of God, while respecting and accepting encounters with God that other followers of Christ reported. They learned to respond effectively to the crucible of enduring challenge.

Any organization that endures faces similar dynamics and challenges. We need centers of integration that can sort through the varied and shared experiences of disparate groups. To overcome our own enduring challenges, we need to embrace communities of faith very different from our own. In the process, we'll see God at work with equal effectiveness.[28]

FOR REFLECTION

1. What are your most prominent experiences of perseverance, and what did you learn from them? About yourself? About others? About God?

2. What has empowered you, and what has hindered you as a result of these experiences of perseverance?

3. What new realities has God awakened in you?

4. How can you work more effectively for purposes greater than yourself?

5. What new experiences leading to fresh understandings have you chosen to ignore?

6. When God made a new, wider understanding known to Peter, God also called Peter to share this new insight at tremendous

cost and sacrifice. Tradition tells us that Peter's call eventually led to his crucifixion. How does your vision for what God is asking you to do require you to expand your understanding of God's work in the world? In turn, how does it require greater perseverance on your part that exceeds the inconvenience?

3

THE CRUCIBLE OF
HUMAN TREACHERY

*While he was still speaking, Judas came, one of the twelve,
and with him a great crowd with swords and clubs, from the chief
priests and the elders of the people. Now the betrayer had given them
a sign, saying "The one I will kiss is the man; seize him." And he came up
to Jesus at once and said, "Greetings, Rabbi!" And he kissed him.*

MATTHEW 26:47-49

*The Lord Jesus on the night when he was betrayed took bread,
and when he had given thanks, he broke it, and said, "This is
my body, which is for you. Do this in remembrance of me."*

1 CORINTHIANS 11:23-24

Et tu, Brute?

JULIUS CAESAR TO BRUTUS AS HE WAS BEING ASSASSINATED

SCRIPTURE AND GREAT LITERARY works abound with examples of human treachery. Throughout this chapter, we consider Judas's betrayal of Jesus in particular. Simply described as "the
night on which Jesus was betrayed," Scripture describes the way in

which Judas set the stage for the governing authorities to capture and eventually crucify Jesus (Matthew 27:11-26; 1 Corinthians 11:23-26). *The crucible of human treachery* involves the suffering that results from the evil action and moral compromises of others.

In "The Inferno," the opening act of *The Divine Comedy,* Dante Alighieri travels through the nine descending circles of hell, guided by the Roman poet, Virgil, the medieval image of human reason. The lowest and ninth circle of hell is reserved for those who commit acts of treachery against those they have a special relationship with. In the final, deepest level of hell dwell traitors, betrayers, and oath-breakers, with the most famous inmate being Judas Iscariot.[1]

Here, in the ninth circle of hell, Satan has three faces (an inversion of the Trinity), one red, one black, and one pale yellow. In each of his three mouths he holds the embodiment of the worst of human nature: Judas in the center, with Brutus and Cassius on each side, the two who plotted and murdered Julius Caesar and triggered the long and catastrophic descent of the Roman Empire.

Throughout my career as a pastor, professor, and college president, I've watched individuals and organizations experience the moral compromise of human treachery and struggle to overcome these difficult challenges. Such experiences strike at the root of a fundamental need of both individuals and communities: the cultivation and reliability of bonds of trust. Personal and corporate flourishing requires anchors of trust in families, communities, and social organizations.

In the early part of the twentieth century, Josiah Royce taught at Harvard University. A native of Grass Lake, California, and an alumnus of UC Berkeley, Royce did his PhD at Harvard under William James, eventually becoming his younger colleague and best friend. Royce talks about the need for "communities of loyalty,"[2] places where we learn how to sublimate our egos to serve purposes greater than ourselves. In the process, we discover how to become citizens of the

"Beloved Community," an enduring community of "truth-centered attitudes and other-centered practices."[3]

Judas's betrayal of Jesus echoes across history because of its startling nature and brutal impact. It reveals the worst of human nature and poses a real and enduring threat to every organization within society—and ultimately to the social fabric of society itself. But it also highlights the need to learn how to read the intentions of others, to pay attention to how human treachery can shape us, and to develop a capacity for self-protection without becoming paranoid. How can we develop these capabilities and understanding?

THE CONSEQUENCES OF HUMAN TREACHERY

Plato once said, "Human affairs aren't serious, but they must be taken seriously; a sad necessity constrains us."[4] The reality of human treachery is much more dire than we often realize. Entire empires and fortunes have been built on human loyalty and destroyed overnight by human treachery and betrayal. The *crucible of human treachery* often compounds the sad state of human affairs. Recognizing that human communities and human flourishing both rely on the capacity for mutual trust, it's essential that we work to engender lasting social connections within our communities and throughout our society.

Behavioral and cognitive psychologists have demonstrated the destructive effects of human betrayal. At its base, human betrayal cultivates anxiety and multiple attachment disorders. It goes on to undermine the confidence and reliability we need in order for our institutions and organizations to run well. At its worst it leads to capital crimes and global wars as public agreements disintegrate. All of these calamities rise and fall on the loss of personal and social integrity and the collective impact from the degradation of common human communities.

In my experience, people are seldom driven by a higher good but are far more often driven by personal benefit, and this motivation is what leads to the temptation, if not the actual behavior, of human treachery in both its individual and collective forms. Researchers define betrayal as the sense of harm from the intentional misrepresentation or misbehavior of a trusted friend, often including the disclosure of sensitive personal information or the deliberate violation of private agreements.[5] The most common forms of betrayal include displays of disloyalty such as harmful revelations of confidential information, infidelity, lying, dishonesty, and acting in deliberately misleading ways. The consequences and effects of betrayal can be traumatic—they can even trigger traumatic episodes in individuals with OCD and PTSD.

SABOTEURS, CHARLATANS, AND THE JUDAS SYNDROME

Across a thirty-five-year vocational career, Rabbi Dr. Edwin Friedman articulates his "Family Systems" approach to organizational leadership.[6] In his most recent work, *Failure of Nerve*, Friedman deals directly with the role of saboteurs and charlatans in emotionally reactive organizations and families.[7] Saboteurs cultivate and replicate triangulation in relationships; in time, there is always a hero and always a villain. Triangulation occurs when two people in conflict draw a third person into the relationship to instigate a new conflict, in order to gain power or influence, or take the focus off the original problem. The leader caught in such a triangle must maintain their relationship and connection while operating with convincing integrity and authority. Otherwise, the organization capitulates to the relational dysfunction.

Likewise, charlatans, although not as destructive, exaggerate their own competence and insert themselves into leadership triangles in hopes of assuring influence. Whether by accident or intent, they end up being called on to give judgment in affairs they're neither competent enough to help resolve nor sufficiently situated so they can benefit from a more mature solution. They seek to stimulate and activate an emotionally reactive system to preserve their place in it. For this to succeed, the principal players must view them as experts— or at least as competent.

Beyond the saboteurs and the charlatans, the Judas Syndrome represents the most treacherous organizational persona. The Judas Syndrome is identified by organizational and behavioral psychologists as the universal tendency to betray other people in order to achieve a desired, self-centered outcome. Contrary to popular belief, the benefits are often closely calculated while the liabilities are often minimized and overlooked. The Judas Syndrome recognizes that fundamentally good people have capacities to do truly awful things.[8]

We seldom pause to think or wonder what led Jesus to choose Judas as a disciple or why couldn't Christ see that he would be the betrayer. We simply assume it must have been the will of God, but Scripture teaches us to pay attention to subtlety and nuance and look deeper. Our tendency as human leaders is to focus on strengths and minimize or neglect weakness. There are some character flaws that are so destructive that no level of gifting is worth putting your leadership at risk. When we realize we have made this mistake, Friedman helps us see that perseverance in the face of sabotage will allow us to rise above our circumstances in order to recover and lead well.

FIVE CAUSES OF HUMAN TREACHERY

Within a systems understanding and approach, the first cause of human treachery is the willingness to deceive in order to advance a personal agenda. This reactive behavior seeks to keep the organization from adjusting and adapting in an attempt to grow, develop, and change. It inhibits forward progress. To overcome this inertia, a leader must discern how to stay emotionally detached from the reacting system while being relationally present and guiding the organization to a new sense of self-understanding and purpose. If not identified and addressed, the reactive behavior leads the organization to continually adapt itself to its most resistant, recalcitrant, anxious members rather than working to fulfill the greater purposes of the organization.

I've experienced this with individuals who are honest but misleading because of what they fail to share. They deliberately underreport a situation to create a false but desirable impression of themselves, another person, or situation. Their unwillingness to disclose the whole situation makes their version completely inaccurate and misleading. I've learned to counteract this tendency by insisting on tracking down the reported behaviors and actions to see if they're accurate before I make a decision about what to do.

A second cause of human treachery is chronic anxiety, which often originates from efforts to grow and change without confidence that an individual or an organization can achieve this goal. Chronic anxiety includes five distinct elements. *Reactivity*, rather than self-regulation. *Herding*, or always giving the least mature, most dysfunctional member control by insisting the group move at the pace of the ones least capable of joining a decision. *Blame triangulation*, which focuses on external individuals or events; in extreme cases, it's a willingness to turn on the individual chosen to lead the group. *Quick-fix mentality*, or the premise that a simple, direct solution exists in highly charged, emotionally complex situations. *Weak or poorly defined leadership*, typified by anxious, ill-defined presence.

In my experience, anxiety leads to human treachery when an individual loses confidence in the path the group or organization has chosen and essentially changes sides. This often results from the influence of a vocal critic the group considers too important to lose. To keep the aggrieved party, the group ignores or downplays ethical compromises. In some cases, the group encourages leaders to take the blame ("throw yourself under the bus") for an event or financial reversal for which the individual bears little or no responsibility.

A third cause of human treachery is an inability to "read the air," due to a preoccupation with data-driven information while paying less attention to relational dynamics.[9] Leaders harm themselves by appearing to be inattentive or tone deaf to dynamics happening around them. In a society preoccupied with data and information, human relationships often suffer as information misleads us into believing we've found excellence or at least certainty. Data-driven decision-making tends to diminish and deny essential emotional processes at the heart of the human interactions that individuals and organizations need to flourish.

I've seen this occur when people on approved paths haven't achieved the results they've imagined. They get feedback suggesting they need to make adjustments, but they don't always receive this information in ways that benefit their strategy. In fact, in many cases of strategic reversal, leaders have been unwilling to listen to negative feedback that should have prompted them to make an appropriate course correction.

A fourth cause of human treachery is what Rabbi Friedman calls the "fallacy of empathy," the way we allow rhetoric to blur the distinction between our personal feelings and sense of offense as opposed to real harm.[10] Individuals accustomed to getting their own way react with all kinds of immature behavior if not allowed to maintain the status quo that rewards or protects them. Here, sabotage shows up as the inability to self-regulate. Malignant members of an organization who fail to see themselves as destructive simply act as they've always done, saying they do what comes naturally. Sometimes, this advocacy provides cover for engaging in insulting behavior that takes direct aim at another person's sensitivities without attempting to create a more positive and life-giving culture.

Ultimately, an effective leader is responsible for holding people accountable for their own behavior, both constructive and destructive. Leaders must push through the tendency to revert to the lowest common denominator. Dysfunctional members of an organization believe they're entitled to force the organization to adapt to their personal preferences rather than joining all the members in serving purposes greater than themselves.

A fifth and final cause of human treachery involves blame triangles that arise for a few well-scripted reasons. First, two individuals or an individual and a group manage their equilibrium by perpetuating their discomfort with one another. Second, blame triangles allow existing relational pathologies to continue. Third, blame triangles permit organizational stagnation to set in, making it difficult for individuals or groups to change their minds so they can grow, develop, and change.[11]

THE DEADLY SIN OF ENVY

Throughout Scripture, different individuals and situations illustrate each of these principles. In John 21, following his resurrection, Jesus goes to Peter at the Sea of Galilee with the ultimate intention of restoring him. What did Peter feel when he saw Jesus, knowing he'd turned against him in his hour of need? And why did Jesus restore Peter and not Judas?

The difference between acts of omission and acts of commission applies here. In Peter's case, he found himself in the wrong place at the wrong time without the inner strength to own his love and loyalty to Christ. He committed an act of omission, and his simple neglect caused significant harm.

By contrast, Judas committed an act of commission, knowingly strategizing to destroy Jesus. I find this tendency to be utterly destructive, both of individual relationships and organizational outcomes. It's symptomatic of what happens to people overrun with envy.

Both the early church and modern psychology pay great attention to the deadly sin of envy. In its milder form, we simply resent the gifts God has given someone else. This kind of envy often prevents us from celebrating and embracing the unique gifts of others—and from learning to accept and embrace the gifts God has given us. While being problematic, it rarely proves destructive.

But there is a deadlier form of envy, *schadenfreude*, which typifies a person so obsessed by their resentment of someone else's gifts that they set out to destroy them. Individuals motivated to commit human treachery have reached a point where they can no longer embrace the gifts God has given someone else and simply want to destroy the individual or their opportunity to make the contribution God intends.

Often, envy results from never coming to terms with the gifts and opportunities God has given us. We may be passed over for a promotion at work, or we've made a contribution that leads to a positive and enduring outcome, but someone else gets the credit. Or we may simply wish we possessed different gifts and abilities. Regardless of what triggers envy, the danger lies in the way it draws us into a black hole of negative energy and sets in motion behaviors that end up destroying us while we seek to sabotage someone else.

Let's consider a few contemporary examples that can help us develop wisdom and insight in order to make a constructive response.

CONFRONTING CHALLENGES WITHIN ORGANIZATIONS

I've served in a variety of midlevel and senior leadership positions that proved to be incredibly rewarding. In every case, they've challenged me and led to significant growth and development. In fact, the growth occurred because of the challenge, but it included discernment about what was really at stake and discipline to do the right thing.

My first example involves a situation my father cautioned me about and encouraged me to avoid: the invitation to be appointed to a job currently held by someone else. Organizations sometimes fall prey to their own processes—or their own sense of self as a professional entity. In this case, the organization carried a general dissatisfaction with the chief executive and this motivated the board to seek a quick solution, believing that they could change the fortunes of the organization for the better with minimal effort or change themselves.

My father cautioned me that what an organization will do to somebody else, they will likely do to you. Pay attention to overtures that come to you from your current position or your prospective position. Friedman identifies the problematic tendencies of organizations that appear in their attitudes and level of support for their leadership. Transitions in leadership always reveal these tendencies, and only a timely and labor-intensive hiring process can identify strengths and confront challenges so an organization can move forward effectively.

In both cases, I chose to decline the positions offered to me and found it incredibly educational to witness this behavior firsthand. I observed improper and proper ways to improve leadership; to achieve this goal we have to proceed in a manner that inspires trust, confidence, and accountability. Otherwise, the damage to the fabric of the organization causes a type of decay that makes it more difficult for future generations of leaders to succeed.

A second example of a challenge within organizations is the willingness to be misleading. In contemporary society, we habitually violate the ninth commandment "thou shalt not bear false witness." In different situations, I've experienced individuals willing to tell a partial account to create a false impression. Early in my leadership development, I gained tremendous insight from Robert Kegan, a leading organizational psychologist and strategist who teaches at Harvard University. In his book, *How the Way We Talk Can Change the Way We Work*, he identifies the importance of recognizing that we never see a total event.[12] We view it from a unique perspective; to gain a complete understanding, we must put our version of events in conversation with additional pieces of the story.

Years ago, on an assignment, I experienced the importance of this reality firsthand when I returned from a business trip and my delayed arrival at the office the next morning was reported to my direct supervisor. The situation itself was easy to resolve: the direct supervisor asked if I had, in fact, come into the office two hours late and if this was a regular practice? I said no, it was not a regular practice, but yes, I had come in two hours late. I also told him that after returning home from a business trip at 2:30 a.m., I'd come into the office at 10:00 a.m. When he heard the rest of the story, he apologized for bringing it up. I was relatively new to this assignment, and we both learned from this experience. I realized I had people who would report incomplete information to my direct supervisor, and my supervisor ended up viewing me and my context with a wider lens. Together, we committed to improving our overall communication so he wouldn't be surprised and I wouldn't feel targeted.

A third example occurs when people triangulate us into a situation because of their own conflict-avoidant personality. Sometimes, individuals with supervisory responsibilities hesitate to communicate tough news in a clear way. This is understandable. American society generally and employment law specifically tend to dictate that communication focused on employment be highly specific and peppered with discrete examples that illustrate the concern. The challenge with this practice, however, is that we often discover that giving even the slightest negative feedback makes an employee feel threatened. They may begin looking for other work or become so demotivated in their position that they become ineffective.

When individuals with supervisory responsibilities don't want to take responsibility for their own judgment and decision-making, they say they're communicating negative information on our behalf. In this case, our triangulation into a supervisory relationship becomes difficult and problematic. Often, we don't even know it has occurred. Occasionally, when we become aware of it, we lack adequate time and resources to correct the record. Friedman emphasizes staying emotionally present while communicating the concerns—this is key. It's the alternative path to triangulation and the only way to ensure an organization can operate at a high level of both integrity and accomplishment.

Finally, be attentive to comparisons, particularly when someone makes an effort to equate our performance with that of an individual who is entirely different. Don't fight the comparison; just show the ways your approach differs so the observer can widen their view of your contribution. Daniel Kahneman talks about our inherent tendency to create mental shortcuts that reinforce our bias.[13] It's natural for all of us to do this, but we need to fight the tendency so we can discern the contribution being made and value it appropriately.

LET GOD BRING LIGHT

Several years ago, I ended up in a situation fraught with misunderstanding. Eventually, the misunderstanding was cleared up, but sometime during the middle of the process, one of the most prominent members of that organization's board invited me to lunch. I wasn't sure what to expect and went hoping for the best, while prepared for a whole range of alternatives.

What resulted was so informative, educational, and developmental. He encouraged me. He showed compassion for me. He wanted to know my version of events. He accepted my explanation that I knew the whole event included me but was bigger than me. We talked for more than two hours. When we finished he prayed for me, looked me straight in the eye, and said, "Walk in righteousness and let God bring to light the cause of the misunderstanding."

Those words have lingered in my mind ever since. So often we feel betrayed by the behavior of others and set out to settle the score, with the end result being a total loss of focus on the responsibilities we carry for our organization and ourselves. When we get drawn into these misunderstandings, they often affect our reputation and leave a lingering cloud over our work.

Conversely, when we let God bring the issues to light, we see his redemptive purposes at work. False accusations evaporate. Clarity of purpose reignites. Our effectiveness grows in dramatic, positive, and life-giving ways. Being misunderstood or even falsely accused is deeply painful. But if we can find within ourselves the inner strength and outer discipline to respond with the mind and spirit of Christ, we can turn potential disasters into opportunities for growth and development that benefit us individually and our organization corporately.

BIBLICAL INSIGHT FROM NEHEMIAH, DANIEL, AND DAVID

Let me offer three examples from Scripture that touch on human treachery and can help illuminate our understanding and guide us. The first one comes from the book of Nehemiah and is filled with examples of how individuals try to stymie renewal efforts by insisting they know what's best. Established opinion leaders in an organization often assert this familiar strategy, intending to counteract any leadership efforts that might generate renewal and reform. In fact, in many cases, a simple desire to maintain their privileged position in a dysfunctional system motivates these individuals.

Throughout the book of Nehemiah, its most famous antagonists, Sanballat, Tobiah, and Geshem, work to counteract Nehemiah by falsely claiming that he seeks to undermine the king. Deliberately working to undermine our direct supervisor is dangerous in any age, but especially treacherous in the days of a monarchy. The possibility of encountering such false claims illustrates an important principle: keep your direct supervisor aware of your regular work. It's a great way to maintain open lines of communication—and a great way to avoid any undesirable surprises. I've discovered that an individual or small group willing to undermine an organization's leader will almost always be willing to undermine you. It's part of the pathology of organizations.

A second example comes from the book of Daniel, in the sixth chapter. This account begins with a description of how Daniel achieved such an elevated leadership responsibility in Babylon. Scripture tells us he had distinguished himself and demonstrated an "excellent spirit" that in turn inspired the confidence of the king. The phrase *excellent spirit* has a variety of meanings, including the inferred capacity to make wise judgments despite the circumstances. In effect, Scripture tells us that Daniel had the unusual capacity to be in any situation, discern the issues, "read the air," and demonstrate sound judgment that inspired confidence in the highest members of society.

Scripture also carefully notes his character: he had never demonstrated any evidence of either corruption or neglect. In effect, Daniel showed up every day, did his job, performed with excellence, and avoided any charge or even suspicion of wrongdoing. He also maintained his love and devotion to God.

Daniel's success led those who served in lesser capacities in King Darius's government to become envious of him. They recognized that all their normal efforts to discredit Daniel wouldn't work. The only successful strategy would be setting up a moral conflict between Daniel's deepest convictions and his relationship with King Darius. These lesser officials achieved their goal and deceived King Darius by instituting an edict that led to an indictment of Daniel. As punishment for his violation of this edict, he's thrown into the lion's den. But Daniel survives this experience. In the end, the officials who attempted to coordinate his demise are the ones who get destroyed. Inevitably, this is what happens to those who resort to strategies driven by envy and deceit.

The final example occurs early in David's adult life when he becomes the target of Saul's schadenfreude. The king has heard the crowds elevating David over himself: "Saul has struck down his thousands, and David his ten thousands" (1 Samuel 18:7). A sitting king with an underdeveloped spiritual life found it challenging to hear David being praised and exalted over him.

David was wise enough to understand that his relationship with Saul had changed. Even though he'd enjoyed the king's favor and still loved his son, Jonathan, like a brother, Saul's schadenfreude had triggered emotions that inevitably led him to seek to capture and destroy

David. Mercifully, God spared David, but the record of the exchange tells the gripping tale of how Saul set out to kill David simply because he could no longer stand for someone to be elevated above himself.

Even today, we sometimes end up working with or for people who are out to destroy us. They may even have been the person responsible for our initial hire, but over time they come to resent our gifts and abilities. As a result, they set out to undermine our opportunity. Ultimately, we need to work for leaders who will focus not on our weaknesses but on our strengths. When we work for supervisors who target us, we end up making mistakes that limit our career and do real harm. As a result, be discerning, recognize your situation, and respond accordingly.

FOR REFLECTION

1. Name a person you thought was an adversary who turned out to be an ally. Why did you misread them? What helped you learn to trust them? How has it influenced you going forward?

2. Name a person you thought was an ally who turned out to be an adversary. Why did you misread them? What caused you to lose trust in them?

3. In your experiences of human treachery, have you encountered more acts of omission or of commission?

4. Are you always an ally or an adversary, or a mix of both? Why?

4

THE CRUCIBLE OF AWAKENED MORAL CONSCIENCE

*The two most important days of your life are the day
you were born and the day you figure out why.*

MARK TWAIN

*If you haven't found something for which
you're willing to die, you're not fit to live.*

MARTIN LUTHER KING JR., JUNE 23, 1963

*Live such good lives among the pagans that,
though they accuse you of doing wrong, they may see
your good deeds and glorify God on the day he visits us.*

1 PETER 2:12 NIV

MARK TWAIN FAMOUSLY OBSERVED that the two most important days of our lives are the day we were born and the day we figure out why. *The crucible that awakens moral conscience is the moment we realize why we were born.* It often involves a pivotal experience or cluster of experiences that coalesce to motivate us to pursue purposes that will outlive us.

On August 28, 1963, Dr. Martin Luther King Jr. delivered his "I Have a Dream" speech on the steps of the Lincoln Memorial in Washington, DC, which many consider the greatest public address in the United States during the twentieth century. A defining moment in the civil rights movement, King's speech helped galvanize support, giving President John F. Kennedy and his brother and attorney general, Robert F. Kennedy, the confidence to push forward on their legislative agenda. It took the coordination of multiple initiatives and the collaboration of widely disparate organizations to make progress on such a grand scale, but momentum had been growing for several years, dating back to the early 1950s. This was King's coming out for America, but when did King realize it for himself?

By his own testimony, it was an evolving, unfolding process similar to the faith journeys and moral awakenings of other great leaders. King himself situated his leadership specifically and the movement generally in the wider understanding of ancient and modern life, drawing from great works of literature, including Scripture. These texts abound with examples of individuals and whole societies who had moral awakenings that changed the course of history. The thought and lives of individuals such as George Washington, Thomas Jefferson, and James Madison animate American history as they experienced similar awakenings during the formation of the United States, the drafting and publication of the Declaration of Independence, and the Revolutionary War.

Later, Abraham Lincoln had a moral awakening regarding the Civil War, the abolition of slavery, and the enduring efforts to keep our country together. The leaders of populist causes throughout the end of the nineteenth and the start of the twentieth century championed a variety of social, spiritual, and cultural awakenings that sought to improve the lives of all Americans. Two world wars brought centuries-old empires to a close as newly formed nation-states emerged as the political order of the day. Winston Churchill, Franklin D. Roosevelt, Dwight D. Eisenhower, and others contributed to the global effort to spread democracy around the world, while the civil rights movement emerged on the domestic front to bring these rights and privileges home.

Elsewhere, individuals such as Dietrich Bonhoeffer and Simone Weil, whose haunting voices echo out of World War II, offered penetrating writings that continue to shape our moral and ethical framework today. Embedded in the German opposition to Adolf Hitler, Bonhoeffer was executed for his role in the assassination attempt on the German leader. Bonhoeffer's abbreviated life produced one of the most compelling approaches to social ethics ever penned.

Likewise, Weil died prematurely and left one of the most original and creative legacies explaining how physical realities (*gravity*) can mediate spiritual ideals (*grace*). "The sun is the only power in the physical universe," Weil begins, "that can get a plant to grow against gravity. Likewise, the love of God is the only power in the spiritual universe that can get a person to grow against the gravity of their own ego." Elsewhere, she amplifies this point by noting,

> The law of gravity which is sovereign on earth over all material motion is the image of the carnal attachment which governs the tendencies of the soul. The only power that can overcome gravity is the sun. . . . We cannot go and obtain this energy, we can only receive it. . . . In the same way, the only effort we can make towards the moral good is to dispose our soul so that it can receive grace, for it is grace which supplies the energy needed for this moral effort.[1]

What a fantastic way to frame our enduring challenge. How do we overcome our dull, fat, relentless ego to awaken morally and engage ethically?

THE MORAL AWAKENING OF MARTIN LUTHER KING JR.

Moral awakenings unfold over time and come to dynamic transition points. American society has entered a second great awakening related to the issue of race. Over the past seventy-five years, we've undertaken an array of approaches to social and cultural challenges to avoid deterioration on the domestic front and another world war globally. During this time, economic growth fueled by stronger political and social cooperation has helped establish a stable world order.

Since World War II, opportunities to make significant and enduring social change have taken root, especially related to race and race relations. These new developments have changed the landscape of American society. But history involves more than the unfolding of inevitable forces or obvious outcomes—it's the combination of great ideas driven by innovative leaders that help a society move closer to fulfilling its governing ideals.

When and where did this new birth of social transformation begin? By the mid-1950s, people started describing the structural and entrenched racism that dominated the southern United States as a cancer eating away at the core of American society. This recognition helped coalesce local and regional forces into a national movement that reshaped the social and political landscape in historic and permanent ways. Combining his innate intellectual gifts and masterful rhetorical powers, King emerged as the movement's leader. His identification, articulation, and consistent embodiment of core, guiding principles provided the moral compass the movement needed as it gained momentum.

Time after time, he combined a keen reading of America's founding documents with core biblical principles, key current events, and a commitment to love and nonviolence that invited all races and ethnicities to participate in the solution. Clayborne Carson, the founding director of the Martin Luther King Jr. Research and Education Institute at Stanford, writes that King's ability to synthesize ideas from a vast array of sources into a meaningful whole rose above his many other gifts. He provided the spirit and the substance that drove the movement. With his creative genius, King created motivating ideals from disparate ideas that propelled social transformation.[2]

King possessed the rare ability to both inspire and convict. Scottish minister James Stewart once said that every sermon should accomplish one of four goals: convince the mind, comfort the heart, motivate the will, or afflict the conscience.[3] In reality, King often achieved all four. His "I Have a Dream" refrain spoke of his hopes not only for Black Americans but also for all Americans. With a conscience awakened to the plight of his own people, he saw racism as a societal flaw and not just a personal evil. He recognized that any sustainable solution had to improve all of American society and not just some of it. Inspired by great philosophical and theological thinkers of the twentieth century, King witnessed the "moral man/immoral society" dichotomy that Reinhold Niebuhr articulated so beautifully.[4]

To counter and overcome this tension, King advocated the need for key leadership from four sectors of American society: executive and legislative politics; White northern liberals; White southern moderates; and strong, courageous leaders from the Black community nationally. He spoke poignantly and persistently about structural racism in the South while pointing out its subtler forms in the North. The South instituted segregation, but the North developed red-lined neighbor-hoods, two-tier credit-rating systems, and carefully crafted public school districts. These "policies" affected every aspect of life, including employment decisions, housing opportunities, and basic education.

REALITIES THAT GUIDED KING

King's amazing intellect combined with his physical and emotional stamina are unparalleled. The ideas he created; the thoughts, books, and speeches he generated; the triumphs he realized; the tragedies he endured; and the miles he traveled represent only some of the hallmarks of his extraordinary life. Here are the guiding realities that molded his character and shaped his destiny.

First and foremost, King was a person of faith and a minister of the gospel of Jesus Christ. When I was coming of age in the 1970s, a great deal of effort went into suppressing this aspect of his life and legacy. Yet King himself repeatedly contextualized his life and effort in the church, where he served as a minister, exemplified devotion as a follower of the life and teachings of Jesus Christ, and celebrated being a child of God. He worked tirelessly to demonstrate how the character of God—both God's justice and mercy—formed the foundation of the civil rights movement.

King sets a great example of how enduring change requires anchoring our efforts to eternal principles. Although religion can be used to stifle progress, more often it serves as an agent of innovation and change. Sincerely held religious beliefs move individuals and motivate whole societies, often knitting together vastly disparate groups in wider communities.

Second, King's natural gift as a great orator contributed to his success. His combined knowledge of vast portions of Scripture, great works of literature, and patriotic stories and songs provided a repertoire he used with magical eloquence to transport our minds and imaginations to a new reality. Historians and biographers have described how King tested new ideas and rhythmic phrases before delivering them to a national and global audience.

Aretha Franklin wrote a moving tribute to King as part of an introduction to a message King delivered at her father's church in Detroit just a few months before the March on Washington. Ahead of the speech at the Lincoln Memorial, he presented familiar themes including his "I Have a Dream" refrain that generated global acclaim while resonating with a national audience.[5]

Likewise, Andrew Young introduced King's last speech from Memphis, "I've Been to the Mountaintop." In this electrifying final oration, King used the simple refrain of the parable of the Good Samaritan to communicate the profound reality that our response to human need changes us for good or ill. Consider this symmetry captured in a moral question. "The priest and the Levite asked, if I stop to help this man, what will happen to me? The Good Samaritan asks, if I don't stop to help this man, what will happen to him?" This latter formulation of the question awakens moral conscience in the form of other-centered love.[6]

When he accepted the Nobel Peace Prize in 1964, King spotlighted the continuing struggle and enduring commitment to embrace love to overcome hate that begets more hate in a vicious, descending cycle leading to self-destruction. He proclaimed, "The need [of our times is] for humans to overcome oppression and violence without resorting to oppression and violence." Identifying the foundation for such a commitment as love, King invited the world to pursue a new path in global relations.[7]

So often we hold ideals only as long as they cause no sacrifice. King embodied the reality that committing our life to ideals that will outlive us always requires sacrifice. But to be capable of sacrifice, we must do the interior, spiritual work that prepares us for trial and challenge.

Third, King combined a warm heart, a keen mind, and a convicted will. Over and over, King pierced to the heart of matters. His unique perspective embraced more than intellectual ideals or spiritual vision. He had the unusual capacity to take ethereal ideas and embody them in a call to immediate action. At a particularly critical turning point in the young history and growing influence of the Southern Christian Leadership Conference, King asked, "Where do we go from here?" He reminded them that when they began ten short years earlier, racial segregation was built into the architecture of southern society. But by 1967, its edifice had been profoundly shaken.[8] This speech reflects King's great vision and his unique capacity to communicate elevating ideals while evoking enduring commitments. As he offered his critique, he also provided a challenge: don't look to Karl Marx, Friedrich Engles, Vladimir Lenin, Leon Trotsky, Ludwig Feuerbach, or any others. None of these relics of history offers the power of God's love that can overcome hate and change the course of history.

King recognized that losing focus and discipline regarding the ideal of love would cause the movement to recede into hate. On numerous occasions, he was the voice of reason in highly charged and reactive situations, helping his colleagues recognize how they would lose the movement's moral authority if they resorted to violence and hate.

A fourth significant guiding reality is that King never wavered on his moral outlook and bedrock convictions. Young reminds us, "No voice more clearly delineated the moral issues of the second half of the twentieth century and no vision more profoundly inspired people as did Martin Luther King Jr.'s dream of American moral possibilities and the universal hope they expressed for humankind."[9] Earlier, in a sermon at the Dexter Avenue Baptist Church, King helped America see that human rights, justice, and nonviolence were tied up in the struggle for freedom, justice, and self-determination.

Countless times, his adversaries—and even more, his allies—pushed, prodded, and tested him. King had that rare ability to tell hard truths without losing an emotional connection. He demonstrates the necessity for a leader to stay emotionally present when a society or an organization experiences rapid change. But it's also the most difficult thing to do well; if we lack the desire for it, we need to rely on discipline.

Fifth, King possessed the amazing capacity to unite disparate groups of people into a national movement. Individuals and schools of thought have emerged elevating or diminishing King, but never ignoring him. As a birthright Quaker, I've marveled at the way he inspired a variety of major Christian denominations to get onboard with his mission and his message, including the Quakers. Nobody ever gets unanimous support, but the effort and energy he expended securing the widest spectrum of participants provides a remarkable testimony to the galvanizing impact of his vision. He also had the unusual grace and humility to say, "Thank you."

King repeatedly highlighted the vast array of organizations and individuals who worked side by side with him. What was it like to experience the presence of his personality and his generosity of spirit and gratitude? Max DePree famously said the first responsibility of a leader is to define reality; the last is to say, thank you.[10] King fully embodied this ideal.

He made a significant impact on me personally and my family of origin, including providing a model for authentic Christian discipleship. Even his nuclear family interested us; we were particularly curious about his four children. We honored King in our home and our church.[11] His standing as an ordained minister, his commitment to nonviolent civil change, and his willingness to espouse American ideals anchored in the love of God that changes the world inspired trust and provided significant credibility. For Christians who believed their faith should shape the public square, King served as a synthesizing voice that promoted nonviolent social engagement while pushing for change that many thought would occur only through social unrest.

King provided the strategic leadership that created the best way forward, a sixth guiding reality. King's life and legacy teach us the essential lesson that nothing gets done without leadership. He illustrates that the priorities and adjustments leaders make in the moment that reflect their vision and values often endure over time. He had no naiveté about the way his efforts created anxiety and unease. People recognized his work as a necessary phase in the nation's growth and development.

Seventh, he demonstrated tremendous savvy politically. King could "read the air" and sense the power and persuasion he carried with the

Kennedy administration. Later, he made even greater inroads by persistently lobbying President Lyndon Johnson. He realized that nothing is real until it becomes local, but nothing local endures unless it becomes policy. These twin realities drove him, and he campaigned tirelessly for the Voting Rights Act and the Civil Rights Act, two pieces of federal legislation that resulted directly from his leadership and effort.

King also had a sense of destiny and recognized that the greatest meaning in life comes from serving God's purposes that will outlive us. "Our feet are tired, but our souls are rested," King said as they completed the march from Selma to Montgomery. "Our aim is not to defeat or humiliate anyone, but to win the friendship and understanding of everyone. It is our hope that everyone will see that the end we seek is a society at peace with itself, a society that can live with its conscience."[12]

King had the singular ability to keep a foot in heaven while planting the other one firmly on earth. He could grapple with the here and now because his view of life had an eternal orientation. He used the vision of the "City of God" to drive the ideals and daily improvements so necessary for the earthly city of humans.

Eighth, King had the remarkable capacity to tie every domestic reality to a global challenge. American struggles had many parallels elsewhere, which he saw as a symbol of hope. He recognized that every nation must rise above its own enlightened self-interest to serve the greater purposes of humankind—the only way forward for humanity and for every individual society. He borrowed the concept of the "beloved community" from Josiah Royce and then expanded it.[13] In addressing the staggering cost and enduring heartache of the Vietnam War, King emphasized the importance of nonviolent social change and his deep commitment to equal rights for all humanity. He offered seven essential reasons for ending the Vietnam War, which he saw as an example of how global violence makes a domestic impact—reasons including violence begetting violence and resources being diverted away from helping the poor at home.[14]

He tied daily struggles to transcendent ideals like truth, justice, equality, and love, a ninth guiding reality of King. The late John Lewis first met King in 1958 when Lewis was an idealistic eighteen-year-old. He writes that King inspired him through his life and prophetic vision as well as the way in which he brought light to such dark places. "After listening to Dr. King, we were so inspired and so moved, we were prepared to march into hell's fires," Lewis said.[15] Elsewhere, King called us to see this individual struggle as a part of a universal struggle because "the arc of the moral universe is long, but it bends toward justice."[16]

The civil rights movement started when Rosa Parks remained in her seat on a city bus. Following her arrest, the subsequent boycott thrust King onto the national stage, and he never wavered. At each juncture, he realized the significance of taking the movement further as it moved beyond the South's regional realities to engulf the national politics of the 1960s. Throughout the struggle, he never wavered in his commitment to make the love of Christ real in the daily lives of everyday people. "Hate begets hate, violence begets violence," King often observed. But he always emphasized that it's "the strong person who cuts off the chain of hate, the chain of evil." King insisted, "Somebody must have religion enough and morality enough to cut hate off and inject within the very structure of the universe the strong and powerful elements of love."[17]

Finally, King's tremendous courage, embodied in his unique and remarkable ability to "bracket out" threats to his life and to his wife and family, made his work possible. In the movement's infancy, someone tried to blow up King's home in Alabama. Thankfully, the bomb malfunctioned. Can you imagine living and working every day with this sort of threat lingering in your mind and imagination? Years later, after multiple threats on his life and the near-death experience of being stabbed by a deranged woman in Harlem, King spoke prophetically about the courage it took to lead the movement and the inevitable destiny for those at odds with the status quo.

Nevertheless, he continued his deep and abiding commitment to nonviolence, unfortunately underestimating the capacity for violence in those who hated him. Less than a year before his assassination, he said, "Today, I stand before you still committed to nonviolence. I am convinced that nonviolence is the most potent weapon available in the struggle for justice in this country."[18] Through the blur and aftermath of his assassination, it was difficult to see nonviolence as the best way. His idealism had guided his purpose in life, but it also left him vulnerable to the enduring reality of human evil.

THE AFTERMATH

In the aftermath of King's assassination, the nation erupted in rioting and protests. Understandable outrage and despair momentarily overran the memory of one who had preached love and nonviolence. But as the air cleared, his colleagues and understudies, companions on his journey, took the torch and began to lead the next phase of the movement's growth and development. Out of the ashes, King's legacy catapulted a whole new generation of leaders and cultural icons who advanced the ideals of freedom and justice. Clayborne Carson of Stanford and Lewis, King's younger friend and understudy, are but two of countless millions who committed themselves to extending King's life and work. This second generation of leadership and political activism has produced a remarkable legacy of positive and enduring change. Before turning to this legacy, let's reflect briefly on some of the great principles and ideas King articulated for us and every subsequent generation.

BIBLICAL INSIGHT FROM ISAIAH 40

King gained inspiration from passages of Scripture and other great works of literature, as well as people of faith and effective leaders. One of his favorite inspirational verses comes from Isaiah 40:4-5 (NIV): There will come a day when "every valley shall be raised up, every mountain and hill made low; the rough ground shall become level, the rugged places a plain. And the glory of the LORD will be revealed, and all people will see it together."

King was aspirational. In the writings of Scripture, he found the voice of God calling him forward. He was remarkable for his ability to live and work in the present while preaching and anticipating a time yet to come.

Theologians talk about the dichotomy of the already and the not yet. King embodied this penultimate state in his very person. Never a complainer, King accepted setback as part of the longer view that guided history and reflected the love and presence of God.

FOR REFLECTION

1. In what way or ways does Isaiah 40:4-5 help you understand King and his ultimate motive? How does it affect you?

2. What other passages of Scripture encompass your ultimate ideals?

3. Many great writers and thinkers deeply influenced King, including Reinhold Niebuhr, the American theologian and ethicist and a prolific writer and frequent guest speaker. For example, King often quoted Niebuhr's observation, "The human [sic] capacity for justice makes democracy possible, but the human's [sic] inclination to injustice makes democracy necessary."[19] How do you respond to this quote? Where do you see it influencing King's life and thought?

4. Dietrich Bonhoeffer in Germany (and briefly in New York City) and Simone Weil in France were doing ethical work before and during World War II. Although not directly involved with King, they influenced him. Weil offered many withering critiques of Western society, including our devotion to mechanized time. In

one of her philosophical essays, she wrote, "On the whole, our present situation more or less resembles that of a party of absolutely ignorant travelers who find themselves in a motor-car launched at full speed and driverless across broken country."[20] Bonhoeffer also saw tremendous problems during the 1930s and early 1940s, yet he advocated that Christians recognize and respond to the circumstances they faced in their everyday life. "The Christian does not live in a vacuum, . . . hence, what the Christian needs is concrete instruction in a concrete situation," he said. "Costly grace . . . is costly because it costs a man his life, and it is grace because it gives a man the only true life."[21] How do the ideas of Weil and Bonhoeffer affect you?

5. What are some of the ways your own moral conscience has awakened, and how has this awakening shaped you?

6. What is your statement of purpose for your life? Here is mine: *to maximize the God-given gifts and abilities of those under my care and influence for the greater good and the kingdom of God.* If you haven't written yours, do so now. Try to keep it to thirty to thirty-five words. Work with a colleague and together write and share your statements with each other.

5

THE CRUCIBLE OF SOCIAL CONFLICT

At a very early stage of the movement, I accepted the teaching
of Jesus, the way of love, the way of nonviolence, the spirit
of forgiveness and reconciliation. The idea that hate is too heavy
a burden to bear. I don't want to go down that road. I've seen too
much hate, seen too much violence. And I know love is a better way.

JOHN LEWIS

About that time there arose a great disturbance about the Way.
A silversmith named Demetrius . . . called them together. . .
and said: "You know, my friends, that we receive a good income
from this business. And you see and hear how this fellow Paul has
convinced and led astray large numbers of people here in Ephesus. . . .
There is danger not only that our trade will lose its good name, but
also that the temple of the great goddess Artemis will be discredited."

ACTS 19:23-27 NIV

Therefore, if anyone is in Christ, the new creation has come: The old has
gone, the new is here! All this is from God, who reconciled us to himself
through Christ and gave us the ministry of reconciliation: that God was
reconciling the world to himself in Christ, not counting people's sins against
them. And he has committed to us the message of reconciliation. We are
therefore Christ's ambassadors, as though God were making his appeal
through us. We implore you on Christ's behalf: Be reconciled to God.

2 CORINTHIANS 5:17-20 NIV

T HE GOSPEL ALWAYS DISRUPTS. It invites us into a life with God and calls us to conduct ourselves so others can experience the presence of Christ when we're present. Unfortunately, Christians don't always succeed in doing this, especially within *the crucible of social conflict*.

On April 29, 1992, riots broke out in Los Angeles after the police officers who were accused of severely beating Rodney King were acquitted. My wife, Pam, and I were living in Orange County, and I had just started a new job at Azusa Pacific University in the San Gabriel Valley. As the riots began, Pam was returning home from a trip to Washington, DC, with the entire eighth-grade class from the school where she taught math. They were scheduled to land at LAX, the huge LA airport, just a few miles south of the epicenter of the riots. The flight was rerouted to Ontario Airport—nearly sixty miles away—but I had already exited the 405 freeway onto Century Boulevard, where an eerie silence engulfed the entire street. I drove as far as the Marriott Hotel near the terminal to pick her up before realizing the final destination of her flight had changed.

When I pulled into the hotel's driveway, security guards waved off cars to prevent people from entering or leaving the hotel. Through the glass doorway, a guard told me to contact the airline to discover my wife's new arrival time and place. After learning she was being rerouted to Ontario, I decided to drive to that airport. As I left the hotel parking lot and reentered traffic, a man began to cross the street. He looked at me and I looked at him, and for that brief moment we both felt a lack of confidence and trust in each other. What would have been an uneventful encounter a day earlier or a month later felt unpredictable and devoid of trust.

The riots resulted in part from the loss of social trust. The acquittal of four police officers who'd been filmed beating King after a traffic stop had enraged those who long felt our justice system neglected them. The incident had begun on one of the many freeways in the sprawling Los Angeles transportation network. The verdict followed an earlier acquittal of Asian shop owners who had killed a Black teenager because the owners believed the teen was shoplifting from their store. These two verdicts destroyed the confidence of an entire community longing for a more just and equitable outcome in both trials.

Nearly thirty years later on Memorial Day in 2020, the world watched in horror as George Floyd suffocated to death while a law enforcement officer in Minneapolis knelt on his neck. The latest in a string of incidents of police brutality, the graphic and unnecessary murder set a nation on fire as protests erupted across the country.

Social unrest born of racial conflict has persisted throughout our history. Older Americans remember the brutal repression of Blacks during the 1960s, while younger Americans know the subtler racism of disproportionate conviction rates and difficulties obtaining even basic goods and services in some parts of our country.

JOHN LEWIS LED BY EXAMPLE

Born on February 21, 1940, in rural Alabama, John Lewis came of age in the early years of the civil rights movement and became a protégé of Martin Luther King Jr. In 2020, shortly before Lewis's death from pancreatic cancer, he returned to the Edmund Pettus Bridge in Selma, Alabama, as part of a documentary featuring his role in the civil rights movement. Fifty-five years earlier, Lewis had been beaten nearly to death for leading a nonviolent march in protest of the forfeiture of voting rights in violation of the Fifteenth Amendment. The broadcast of this unprovoked attack added to the rising tide of moral and po-litical outrage sweeping America.

Having suffered a fractured skull and multiple lacerations, Lewis recovered, went on to be arrested forty-five times for civil disobe-dience, and finished his life's work as a US congressman. He often marveled at how much had changed in the country for the better, while recognizing how far we still needed to go. Like his mentor, Lewis was deeply motivated by the life and teachings of Jesus and saw in the country's plight the same pilgrimage from sin to redemption that he experienced as an individual. Lewis also believed in sin but never used it as an excuse. Eventually, *Time* magazine labeled him a saint—not perfect, but fully committed to a way of life.[1]

Lewis was an idealist with a realist bent. He recognized that Christianity had been used as a means of repression, but he believed more strongly that it served as a great weapon of liberation and change. Like King, he embraced religious devotion, echoing Alexis de Tocqueville's belief that it repressed "a multitude of petty, passing desires" to achieve an ultimate and enduring ideal.

Few other voices in the civil rights movement both preached the principle and enacted the practice as consistently as Lewis. He lived with hope, always looking to the next horizon. He saw all they'd overcome as signposts on the way to justice and freedom. He carried King's vision of hope for a better America, living with the dream of a "beloved community" that fulfilled the Christian concept of the kingdom of God on earth.

Ultimately, King and Lewis found solace in the great tradition of Saint Augustine, who recognized human evil but also understood how God fulfills his purposes in and through history. Lewis, like King, never wavered in his confidence and belief in the Christian message and the practices of mercy, forgiveness, and compassion buoyed by the virtue of hope.

SOCIAL CONFLICT ON CAMPUS

I first encountered the crucible of social conflict while growing up in Eugene, Oregon. By the time I was ten, the local news cycle prominently featured University of Oregon students planning and participating in civil rights protests, fire-bombing the ROTC building near campus, and speaking out regularly and aggressively against the Vietnam War. President John Kennedy, Robert Kennedy, and Martin Luther King Jr. had all been assassinated. Some of those creating turmoil in the country through their peaceful, nonviolent activism were driven by a desire to make the United States a better place, extending to every American the opportunity to realize in their own life the reality of our founding ideals. Unfortunately for others, hatred and animosity overran their allegiance to more noble purposes.

More than fifty years later in 2020, I was leading Westmont College as we confronted a new wave of shortcomings and unfulfilled promises as a society despite positive developments and changes on many fronts. Because social media provides visual images in real time, we sometimes feel numb or even overwhelmed by brutal realities from halfway around the world. This callousness not only deadens us to world calamities, it paralyzes us in the face of equally painful but more hidden realities closer to home. As we witnessed firsthand the murder of George Floyd, we saw the growing animosity and then the deepening disillusionment as well-intentioned protests turned violent and destructive.

During this time, we also began to hear reports about how we could have done better as a college with more accurate depictions of life on campus for underrepresented groups, more authentic conversations about race, and even better advising. As the global realities of racial unrest collided with the local experiences of bias and neglect, we found ourselves relying on some old friends while also reaching for new help.

Several important voices stepped into this cauldron of discontent offering hope, help, and counsel. Pastors, professors, and cultural leaders all provided great insight and effective strategies. We began a broad-based review as a college and a community. We intensified efforts already underway in a desire to make positive changes that helped us fulfill our mission. George Yancey, a sociologist who teaches at Baylor University in Texas, became one of our most significant talking partners.

Yancey has been working for his entire career on issues of racial justice, reconciliation, and diversity. Two of his works are especially important. One of these, *Neither Jew Nor Gentile: Exploring Issues of Racial Diversity on Protestant College Campuses*,[2] is one of the best books in the field, providing both insight and guidance about constructively addressing issues of race at faith-based colleges.

He describes his method as "mutual accountability" and defines it as "a Christian-based approach whereby we recognize that people of all races have a sin nature that has to be accounted for. Therefore, everyone has an obligation to work toward healthy interracial relationships and community."[3]

ESTABLISHING DIVERSITY PRIORITIES

Yancey fleshes out the ideals of his program by articulating four main priorities; I offer here the ways in which we are applying each one. In each case, the goal is to come up with strategies that include remedies for all elements of our constituency.

Increasing diversity on campus by hiring faculty of color who fit the college's mission. Standing commitments and entrenched realities make quick changes in faculty composition difficult. The average professor works at a college or university for thirty or more years if they achieve tenure. Westmont, with a capped enrollment, has approximately one hundred full-time faculty positions. Change occurs only through non-tenure renewals, retirements, or new academic programs. Until recently, we had limited ability to develop new programs due to our enrollment cap. We could hire people of color only through retirements and non-renewals. Nevertheless, we continue to seek faculty and administrators of color who align with our mission. Because of this commitment, we're able to recruit persons of color highly trained in their field and committed to our faith-based mission. These efforts and decisions give us an opportunity to make tangible and enduring impacts on the composition of our faculty. They also reflect the multifaceted efforts it takes to deliberately pursue deeply held commitments that positively affect our community's culture.

Hiring a diverse faculty leads to diversifying the curriculum, offering courses and educational experiences that go beyond the Western canon. During the spring and fall of 2020, we implemented several new courses, planned and established new majors and minors, and created slots for visiting professors from diverse backgrounds. This, too, is a challenging but essential strategy. Because of a capped enrollment, we're constantly juggling faculty workloads to offer under-enrolled courses required for majors and minors. These innovations have laid the groundwork for us to do even more as we move beyond the restrictions imposed by the global pandemic. We're managing our way through the new challenges of millions of young adults who've elected to drop out of college—while also developing new programs like engineering and nursing that provide new opportunities moving forward.

After diversifying, work to establish multicultural, student-led organizations that create positive experiences for students from underrepresented groups. Another reality faces those responsible for creating positive experiences for students from a variety of diverse backgrounds. This type of change often requires several offices to work together, including my own. Individuals effectively aligning their new programming with our enduring mission are succeeding in building bridges with all sectors of the Westmont community. These efforts have created multiple opportunities to influence the college culture and to foster intercultural exchanges. Our strong global studies program complements this work because we encourage students to spend a semester in a culture other than their own. As explained in chapter one, we've developed a three-fold cycle of global learning, which has provided the experience and the guided learning in order to understand how to engage and exegete the vast array of cultures that comprise our global community. Acquiring this competency isn't a cure-all, but it does help prepare students for the increasingly diverse world they'll face as we move deeper into the twenty-first century.

To ensure a holistic approach, develop programs that also work with students from the majority culture to draw them into positive experiences with faculty and students of color, making them part of the overall process and solution. As Yancey's unique focus amplifies, we need to incorporate students from the majority culture in these endeavors. In this way, we embrace the importance of valuing every member of a community in order to develop an enduring solution. It communicates a cultural value of inclusion and also creates an expectation.

As a result, we've provided a variety of resources and experiences to build a foundation for a common conversation. Strategic partners assisting us include Mosaix, based in Little Rock, Arkansas. Originally started by Mark DeYmaz and now led by Senior Pastor Harry Li, this church-based ministry has partnered with the Cultural Intelligence Center and developed into a global leader on issues of race, culture, and Christianity. Another important partner, David Bailey and Arrabon, a ministry based in Richmond, Virginia, has helped us make important headway on a number of fronts through their general work and their specific workshops on "Language Matters." Both Harry and David have the unusual gift and ability to speak across a variety of cultural boundaries to help us understand social dynamics so we can craft common commitments that improve our community.

Finally, we've started a program, Compelling Conversations, that features interviews with people of color who are personal friends and leading thinkers about culture, including those from our own college and surrounding community. These resources help us hear from a multitude of voices that have not always enjoyed a platform, giving us insight into the stories of those who often work without much fanfare or notice. Other efforts include inviting current students and alums from underrepresented backgrounds to tell their stories. We've heard about what we did well and ways we could have done a lot better.

These four guiding priorities have helped us begin our response to the cultural moment, recognizing it's just the beginning and will need to be an enduring commitment in the years ahead. Additionally, growth and change are part of God's grand design for life on earth. Reconciliation between differing factions is not only a necessity but also a desired reality. Efforts at reconciliation recognize that every new generation must grow in its capacity to extend understanding and care throughout the earth.

CHARTING THE WAY FORWARD

A second work by Yancey helps us strive for the next level. A great sequel, *Beyond Racial Division: A Unifying Alternative to Colorblindness and Antiracism*,[4] provides sound strategy and guidance. This latest installment threads the needle between two alternative responses that fall short of adequately accounting for the realities impeding constructive and enduring progress while building on the approach of mutual accountability. Drawing on his experience of healthy interracial communication and community, Yancey suggests that both colorblindness and antiracism result in "racial alienation," which keeps us from addressing and resolving issues that create distrust, perpetuate racism, and keep our communities in turmoil. He believes the only sustainable solutions are ones that take the dignity, value, and worth of every individual seriously.

On the one hand, Yancey sees colorblindness as ignoring the huge realities of racism both past and present. On the other hand, he sees antiracism as intensifying racism by giving both implicit and explicit permission to treat certain racial groups disrespectfully. He considers both alternatives inadequate. With his emphasis on "mutual accountability," Yancey seeks to welcome and listen to every voice. Ultimately, his approach invites full participation by all individuals and communicates a value for humans unusual for these conversations. Yancey is a unique and original voice working in the tradition of Martin Luther King Jr., John Lewis, and other great civil rights leaders.

To better understand both the nature of the issue and how we can respond constructively and deepen our engagement, we've found additional approaches helpful.

We began by building a network of conversation partners for the primary reason the issue mattered to our community even though we fell short on a variety of fronts. We've learned it's important to build these networks simply because it's the right thing to do and will give us wider insight into the realities we all face culturally and organizationally. This priority helps us develop the capacity for empathetic listening, pursue bridge building, participate in initiatives bringing subgroups together for greater understanding, and encourage growth in social norms and mores so these conversations across groups can lower barriers, cross boundaries, and diminish explicit and implicit bias.

It's essential to understand the macro-environment in which we work and minister. Robert Putnam and Shaylyn Romney Garrett offer an outstanding resource for this in their classic, *The Upswing: How America Came Together a Century Ago and How We Can Do it Again*.[5] The authors present a hypothesis that outlines a 125-year sweep of American history they describe as an "I-We-I" curve. It's best understood by seeing the dynamic interplay between economic inequality, political polarization, social isolation, and cultural narcissism. Putnam and Garrett add race and gender to these four disorienting realities, defining and amplifying six areas to help us understand how we've reached the nadir of this social, cultural, economic, and historic moment while expressing hope for a gradual recovery through another great upswing.

By economic inequality, Putnam and Garrett mean the vast discrepancies of wealth between sectors of the global economy such as the tech and finance multimillionaires and billionaires and the stagnant wages of most other Americans. They describe political polarization as the loss of negotiated compromise as both a pragmatic ideal and a governing reality. They define social isolation by going back a generation, when Robert Bellah highlighted the start of this trend by documenting and commenting on the retreat of Americans into "lifestyle enclaves." The dynamics of cultural narcissism have been well documented and widely critiqued. Complementary public intellectuals like David Brooks have captured this same trend by examining the difference between people driven by "resumé virtues" and those guided by "eulogy virtues," enshrined by self-giving sacrifice that focuses on others rather than promoting ourselves.[6]

The final two, race relations and gender equality, highlight similar patterns of unprecedented advances through the early 1970s only to encounter reversals and declines in the past fifty years. Putnam and Garrett effectively show the many ways Black people were moving toward parity with Whites well before the victories of the civil rights movement. But these trends began to slow in the 1970s, and in many cases even reversed in subsequent years. Similar patterns occurred with efforts for women to achieve gender equality. Together, these six areas encompass critiques of major social, cultural, and political developments that have marked America as we've tried to fulfill our commitments both to individual achievement and community support.

WHAT CAN I DO?

We've also sought to engage micro-strategies that fit our cultural moment and our organizational life cycle. Yancey offers several suggestions in his books. So do other leading cultural thinkers. The main point is finding resources that will best help your organization and then deploying them. Yancey seeks to get everyone involved as part of the solution. By working together, we honor the dignity, value, and worth of every individual, communicating fundamental respect for all. As people grow, their opinions shift and change. So will our organizations. Keep the conversation going by cultivating a variety of new and relevant resources as you work to enculturate each new generation.

Then focus on continuous improvement by consulting experts and respecting their advice without losing a sense of how best to apply their input to your organization. Avoid two equally strong and polarizing tendencies: going it alone or capitulating to every new opinion. Both leave an organization unmoored from its core mission and adrift in a sea of multiple voices, lacking clear direction.

Another priority must be committing to work for real change. Tell your story without engaging in empty virtue signaling or narcissistic self-promotion. Over time, your record speaks for itself. Combine a curiosity for the stories of others with a sincere sharing of your own spiritual and intellectual journey. For example, Martin Luther King Jr. matters a great deal to me, not only for his achievements as a civil rights leader, but because the Quaker religious community in which I grew up elevated his message and approach. He was truly a cultural and spiritual thought leader to my religious community.

Increase your impact by helping build centers of integration in our society so greater understanding and knowledge can emerge. Historically, competitive athletics and the military have been two primary centers of social integration in America. But several social critics continue to highlight the loss of predictable avenues of social integration and the consequent fraying of American society. Everyone from Robert Bellah[7] in the 1980s to James Davidson Hunter and Robert Putnam more recently decry the demise of cross-community conversation.[8] These sociologists and cultural leaders note the fracturing of centers of integration in American culture and emphasize the need to find new ones that can guide us. As we move deeper into the twenty-first century, churches, voluntary associations, and community centers are re-emerging as areas that many hope will provide mutual footing for multiracial initiatives and conversations. Be a part of initiatives that restore and strengthen America's social fabric.

Finally, read American history with an honest appraisal of its strengths and its limitations. As one Black pastor from Tampa, Florida, said to me on a Zoom call, "I didn't need critical race theory to tell me systemic racism exists in America. Just read a full account of American history, and you can see it." Studying American history with a wider lens also helps us develop a respect and appreciation for heroes and heroines we haven't properly honored and respected.

Rarely if ever do the crucible of natural disaster and the crucible of social conflict overlap, but that's what we face today. We're realizing that as we respond to one, we can learn how to better approach the other. Every day during the pandemic of 2020 we knew we had to take incredible care in how we lived and interacted to limit and minimize the spread of the coronavirus. While it was tiring and draining, it was the only way to work with any hope of experiencing a semblance of normal life. It's also how we showed compassion and care for the vulnerable populations in our midst. We had an opportunity to learn how to be empathetic to the needs of others, which helps us respond with a spirit reminiscent of Jesus when we encounter issues arising from the crucible of social conflict.

On that visit to the Edmund Pettus Bridge, several colleagues of the civil rights movement offered their reflections on the day, including a final observation by John Lewis. All who had been alive and active during that period had seen so much during their adult lifetime. Lewis remembered the moment as a signpost to a greater reality. "Some of us gave a little blood that day," he began, "in order to redeem the soul of America."

BIBLICAL INSIGHT FOR THE MINISTRY OF RECONCILIATION

In 2 Corinthians 5, Paul instructs us to engage fully in a ministry of reconciliation. He recognizes that in his Roman and Greek world, society often saw a Christian long before they saw Christ. Likewise, his exhortation to be ambassadors for Christ reminds us to take a moral inventory of our own life and ask, "Do I really respond empathetically and compassionately to the needs of those around me?" The crucibles we encounter offer opportunities for us to grow in our love and understanding of God. Conversely, they can also distract us from this growth if we let them. The response we make will fundamentally determine whether the crucibles affect us for good or ill.

Like their impact on us, crucibles that affect us simultaneously touch others. It is a recognition that the response we make to the "total event" will fundamentally determine whether the outcome bears enduring fruit. While our commitment to reconciliation extracts a toll on us, it pays rich dividends by helping produce good in others.

FOR REFLECTION

1. What new religious movements driven by reformation and renewal have fundamentally changed the trajectories of various societies and cultures?

2. When you read his life history[9] and watch the TV biography *Good Trouble*,[10] what do you conclude motivated Lewis to work tirelessly for social and political reform?

3. What experiences and exposures have changed your outlook and motivated new behavior?

4. If we take cultural understandings depicted in Acts 19 and invert them, what innovations did the first Christians introduce that embraced human flourishing?

5. What passage of Scripture describes a specific cultural and social experience you've had, and how do you understand and respond to it?

6. What new understandings have you developed about how God wants you to behave in our contemporary society?

7. When you consider the "I-We-I" curve identified and articulated by Putnam and Garrett, do you agree or disagree with it, and how can you respond in light of your understanding?

8. What can we do to engage constructively in efforts to improve our community specifically and our society generally?

6

THE CRUCIBLE OF
HUMAN SUFFERING

For he makes his sun rise on the evil and on the good,
and sends rain on the just and on the unjust.

MATTHEW 5:45

I thank my God every time I remember you . . . with joy because
of your partnership in the gospel from the first day until now,
being confident of this, that he who began a good work in you
will carry it on to completion until the day of Christ Jesus.

PHILIPPIANS 1:3-6 NIV

Consider it pure joy, my brothers and sisters, whenever you face
trials of many kinds, because you know that the testing of your
faith produces perseverance. Let perseverance finish its work so
that you may be mature and complete, not lacking anything.

JAMES 1:2-4 NIV

D R. STORY WOULD LIKE TO SPEAK WITH YOU," the note
said. "He's available after your afternoon class today. Please stop
by his office." In October 1982, I'd just started at Princeton Theological

Seminary, and Dr. Story taught my New Testament Greek class. I wondered about the cryptic message from my academic adviser—I'd completed all my assignments and was doing well in his class. The meeting later that afternoon began with brief pleasantries, then he quickly moved to why he'd asked to see me. My mentor Don Green had suffered a tragic accident on Mount Hood and was clinging to life after being airlifted to a Portland hospital. He'd been collecting firewood on the western slope near the Zig Zag ranger station.

The news shocked and devastated me. We hoped that Don would survive, but he eventually succumbed to his catastrophic injuries, leaving behind a wife and four small children. I was numb. I'd come to Princeton because Don had attended the seminary ten years earlier. Dr. Story had advised him, and now he was guiding me—he encouraged me to reach out to Diogenes Allen, Stuart Professor of Philosophy at Princeton. He'd just finished a book on the nature of evil and suffering, exploring how we could understand it and make a redemptive response.[1]

This singular recommendation began a friendship that continues to influence me more than ten years after Dr. Allen died of non-Hodgkin's lymphoma in 2013. He mentored me, strengthening my Christian faith and giving me the confidence to believe Christianity could hold up in the marketplace of ideas. Most importantly, he helped me make sense of evil and suffering rather than sidestepping this difficult issue.

Rabbi Harold Kushner published a popular response to suffering in his 1981 book, *When Bad Things Happen to Good People*.[2] This perennial *New York Times* bestseller presented a pastoral and practical approach that touched millions. Some of these ideas were taken from the rich heritage of Christian responses to evil and suffering across the two-thousand-year history of the church. Combining Kushner's brief treatise with key works from Christian history produces a response to evil and suffering that is relevant, pastoral, and life-giving.

THEODICY: MAKING SENSE OF A LOVING GOD AND THE REALITY OF EVIL

All my life, I've wondered about the meaning and purpose of evil and suffering. Some of my earliest memories include struggling to understand why so many people could do such horrible things to other humans, often those they were obligated to love. Evil and suffering at the hands of nature also puzzled me. For five years, I relentlessly pursued questions about how a loving God could allow so much suffering, a part of my larger quest to determine whether Christianity was, in fact, true.

This process, known as *theodicy*, attempts to reconcile an all-good, all-powerful, all-loving God with our experiences of evil and suffering. Scripture and Christians throughout church history have wrestled with this issue. The book of Job attempts to answer the question of why do bad things happen to good people? Job asks God why sixteen times. Jesus says the rain falls on the just and the unjust alike (Matthew 5:45).The apostle Paul anchors the mysteries of life to the sovereignty of God, essentially saying "who are we to question the will of God?" Other writers—like Irenaeus in the second and early third century, Saint Augustine in the fourth and early fifth century, Aquinas in the thirteenth century, Blaise Pascal in the seventeenth century, and Austin Farrar, John Hick, and Diogenes Allen in the twentieth century—have all offered compelling explanations about how we can simultaneously love and understand God and respond redemptively to evil and suffering.

Don's tragic accident was my first tangible experience of suffering due to the death of someone dying relatively young, seemingly out of sequence. This disruption prompted me to seek help in understanding how to put such disorienting experiences into a wider framework of meaning so I could live with these realities without being destroyed by them. What are some of these realities, and what resources help us make an enduring response?

EXAMPLES FROM SCRIPTURE, CHRISTIAN WRITERS, AND EXPERIENCE

Recently, I was studying the prison epistles in the New Testament, pondering the challenges the first Christians faced as they built the early church. A thought overwhelmed me: *How did Paul keep such an upbeat attitude in the midst of all his suffering?* I returned to Jesus' words in the Gospels and to the general epistles and began thinking even more broadly: *How did the entirety of the early church find such strength and courage to carry on in the face of persecution, even to the point of death?*

Years ago, as I was reading Walker Percy novels, one of his observations addressed the heart of my question: "There are really only two types of people," Percy wrote. "Those for whom life is a quest, and those for whom it isn't."[3] I've discovered that people who see life as a quest find admirable and truly transformative ways to persevere in the face of hardship.

This insight helped me realize that dealing with crucibles requires embracing life as a quest rather than seeing hardships as unnecessary intrusions or complete disruptions. I began to accept evil and suffering as part of the human experience. These realities are not signs of God's abandonment of us. Instead, they serve as signposts guiding us to make sense of suffering, a reality every generation must face.

Earlier, I used two beautiful analogies Simone Weil offers in *Gravity and Grace* that help us understand both how we awaken morally and also how we can respond constructively to suffering.[4] She compares the love of God to the power of the sun. Just as the sun enables a plant to defy gravity and grow upward, so the love of God allows us to grow against the power of our own egocentrism. Weil suggests that the first step in dealing adequately and accurately with experiences of evil and suffering is recognizing that we often view them from their impact on us personally. To understand them accurately, we must move beyond the power of our "dull, fat relentless ego."

The second challenge is our tendency to view evil and suffering as barriers to God rather than divine passageways. Although philosophers and skeptics cite experiences of evil and suffering as impediments to belief, people who really suffer often become open to the possibility and reality of the love of God. As a grief recovery counselor, my wife, Pam, has the incredible privilege of helping people come to terms with some of the most painful, disorienting experiences of their lives. She recognizes that at moments of profound loss, people almost universally look for help through the spiritual reality of God.

While a seminary student at Princeton, I studied the Old Testament with Bernhard W. Anderson, especially his work on the Psalms of lament.[5] He helped me understand the application of these passages to human suffering. The structure of these laments moves beyond naturalistic explanations that stop short of including God,[6] instead, they feature a six-fold pattern:

- addressing God

- complaining about what bothers the psalmist

- expressing trust and confidence in God

- petitioning God specifically

- using words of assurance and confidence that God hears and will respond to the complaint

- vowing to praise: the promise to recognize God's provision

I've found this structure helpful because it allows us to complain but also directs us to see God's presence as we endure our travail. Recognizing that the reality of evil and suffering raises a hurdle to Christian belief, we need to create a structure of meaning, or a mental map, that helps us locate God and our belief in him within the wider framework of our experiences of life. It's possible to see in the material universe a breathtaking and awe-inspiring beauty. We can also recognize that the beauty and grandeur of creation operates without regard for its impact on human life. This doesn't discount the existence of God, but it calls for a meaningful and coherent response to demonstrate how a loving God could create a universe with natural disasters, terminal illness, and human cruelty.

NATURAL DISASTERS

During our time at Westmont, we've responded to several crucibles forged by natural disasters, beginning with the Tea Fire in November 2008. A group of ten students from another institution in Santa Barbara reportedly started a small fire the night before at the Tea Gardens, an area directly above our campus. They put it out with sand and dirt but failed to anticipate the strong, sundowner winds that occur every fall in Southern California. The next afternoon, the winds picked up, and shortly before 6:00 p.m., the smoldering embers exploded into a raging fire that swept onto campus.

The college had trained and practiced for evacuations to the gym in the event of a wildfire, but we'd never had a blaze ravage campus so quickly and so devastatingly. Thankfully, the strategy of sheltering in place worked as everyone evacuated safely, and we rode out the fire. Although the blaze destroyed eight buildings on campus, one million square feet of vegetation, fifteen faculty homes next door, and more than two hundred homes in the neighborhood, no lives were lost. We learned from this disaster that preparation is essential to minimize damage and prevent any loss of life. The Tea Fire led us to make a positive, pro-active, life-affirming response and start our own volunteer fire department, purchase firefighting trucks and equipment, and train members of our buildings and grounds crew to be first responders on campus. We then rebuilt and repopulated the campus, maintaining an environment most likely to mitigate a fire.

At the opening of the book, I mentioned the second and third disasters. The Thomas Fire of December 2017 started forty air miles east of Santa Barbara and crept along the ridgeline of the Santa Ynez Mountains, arriving right above campus ten days after igniting. This inferno baked the ground like clay in a firing kiln. For several days, crews of five hundred firefighters with one hundred full-size fire trucks bivouacked at Westmont. As the fire entered our community, various crews hopscotched down the ridgeline, fighting flames that reached the edge of campus. Although we suffered minimal damage to buildings and landscape, the fire created conditions that resulted in the Montecito debris flow early on the morning of January 9, 2018.

This third, monumental disaster, both in its initial devastation and its ongoing tragedy, affected only those in harm's way. I had awakened shortly before 3:00 a.m. and was making coffee in our kitchen when a torrential downpour started. The loud pounding awoke our daughter Liz, who had just returned from a social entrepreneurship internship in San Francisco. She joined me in the kitchen, and we went into the backyard to see if we could figure out what was causing a translucent red flame that danced against the canopy of high-level clouds.

I feared that yet another fire had started and would threaten campus. I never thought we were seeing a broken natural gas line, the first dramatic consequence of the debris flow. To make the best possible judgment about the potential threat, I asked Liz if she'd get in the car and help me try to determine the flame's proximity to campus. We drove down Cold Spring Road, turned left onto Sycamore Canyon Road, and traveled just a few hundred yards down the road before we had a premonition that we should return home. Without knowing it, we'd come within a few hundred yards of one of the tributaries carrying the debris flow to the ocean.

Later that morning, we began learning the human toll. Dear friends and complete strangers lost their homes, and some even lost their lives. Our daughter Anna became a frontline caregiver for a family who suffered the death of two members and the destruction of their home. I witnessed the incredible strength that comes when a person is willing and able to be emotionally present to people who have experienced the worst form of suffering and loss. People suffer stages of trauma, just like with grief. We can meet, embrace, endure, and ultimately

complete these stages if companions help us work through our tragedies. We come to realize that although everyone can heal, each individual experiences their own time frame for healing. We have to allow
the spirit of each person to set the pace.

The global pandemic, the fourth and final disaster, began to affect
us in March 2020. As the racial conversations opened up, the world
began to shut down. Nobody knew for sure how best to navigate the
virus. Disputes raged on every front, from national news networks to
local community email threads. Some saw it as a conspiracy while
others considered it a deliberate attack. Those working to minimize
its human toll and global fallout looked to science for a cure.

Covid-19 presented a huge challenge to people working on the
frontlines in human-centered, community-facing organizations. We
finished the 2019–2020 academic year via Zoom. During the time we
moved from studying on campus to learning on screens, the cultural
conversation seemed to ebb and flow depending on personalities and
perspectives. But the tragic and highly publicized murder of George
Floyd on Memorial Day supercharged the conflict and the discussion.
We couldn't sidestep these issues as we responded to the pandemic.
The college had to continue operating, and we had to figure out a way
to open back up in the fall.

As we worked our way through summer, we combined preparation
for the return of students with our response to social conflict, as I
described earlier. We found our experiences with the fires and debris
flow gave us incredibly helpful institutional expertise as we worked
with the county public health officer and multiple constituencies in
our community. We learned a critical lesson: use the disasters we
experience both to recover and to build institutional resilience that
will help us in the future. Organizations and individuals benefit from
opportunities to learn and grow, but we need to be open to these opportunities and be engaged in ways that help our constituency respond to whatever crucible occurs.

SUDDEN DEATH AND TERMINAL ILLNESS

My father died in 1989 of a heart attack when he was sixty, and my mother died in 2003 of ovarian cancer at the age of seventy-three. Both were incredibly supportive of me, and I found their deaths difficult for different reasons. The night before my father died, Pam and I had driven to Eugene and enjoyed a delightful dinner with my parents and a wonderful early morning conversation with my father. He wanted to know about our current challenges and our future dreams. Always an optimist, he saw opportunities instead of challenges—he didn't believe challenges kept us from our ultimate destiny.

Although emotionally devastating, the death of Don Green seven years earlier and the work I'd done to understand a loving God in a world filled with evil and suffering helped prepare me for my father's death. If we let it, death can teach us a lot; it humbled me. I learned that we don't always realize our desires, but they point us to our hopes and dreams and how to respond when they remain unfulfilled. I served as a pastor at the time, and I remember noticing an aging couple alienated from all three of their adult children when I returned to the congregation. I could hardly imagine how much more difficult my circumstances would have been if estrangement had complicated our grief.

My mom's death was different. Born to hardship and raised in adversity, she developed a reserved demeanor that always assumed a reversal of fortune. If my dad believed everything inevitably worked out, my mom believed everything eventually fell apart. Diagnosed in May 2001, she died twenty-two months later in March 2003, after undergoing major surgery, chemo, a period of remission, and then a devastating return that led to her death. My shock and turbulence from my father's death had given way to seeing death as a blessing, relieving my mother's suffering by releasing her into the hands of God.

I came to see how unremitting suffering causes a person to long for a life beyond death. The grief I shared with my siblings, as well as other relatives and friends of my mother, helped me realize how positive memories rise to the surface of our memory and bring comfort. God uses our experiences to console and assure us.

The death of my parents taught me such a profound lesson because neither one lived to a natural end. My desire that they survive couldn't thwart the reality of evil and suffering due to sudden death or terminal illness.

HUMAN EVIL

We also experience evil and suffering at the hands of other humans. My first year in seminary, Elie Wiesel spoke on campus, creating a moving and memorable event. The author of *Night,* Wiesel embodied the incredible effort to take the horrifying experiences of the Holocaust and redeem them for higher purposes. He was humble, eloquent, and noble. A perfect spokesperson for this horrific period of human history, he helped restore a moral outlook on a dark period in his own amazing way.[7]

At the time, I was reading Viktor Frankl's book *Man's Search for Meaning.*[8] Based on his experiences of the Holocaust, Frankl wrote poignantly about the necessity of finding the "why" in our suffering to endure any "how." Through their writings, both authors make an enduring contribution that helps us see the redemptive outcome of a human response to experiences of profound evil. How we respond to evil completes the cycle and keeps it from destroying us.

In chapter three, I wrote about the catastrophic impact of envy, and especially schadenfreude, as these inner motives work to destroy personal dreams and ruin human communities. When it takes a barbaric turn, acts of human evil lead to atrocities on an unimaginable scale.

As I write, the world focuses on the unprovoked war in Ukraine, where human atrocities are reported daily. The suffering recalls the darkest periods of the previous century. How could the light of civilization and social progress have grown so dim? Regardless of our perspective, we all agree that innocent suffering deserves to be stopped. We also wonder if the global order will hold. Can we make progress so people carry out the right policies in the right way for the right reason? Can we find a way to respond to human evil without destroying our own soul in the process? What strategies invite a creative and redemptive response?

The worst suffering occurs from human evil and cruelty, which strikes at the heart of our humanity and reflects the intrusion of a culture of death into our modern era. The reality of this age-old evil always destroys, demoralizes, and endures. But one of the ways that redemption can come to us is through art.

ART AND TRANSCENDENCE

During my three years at Princeton Seminary, I had an intellectual awakening and developed a deep love and interest in great works of art, especially by famous painters. On one of my many excursions to Washington, DC, I visited the National Gallery of Art and spent four hours in the area featuring select works by some of the most famous impressionist artists. I had an opportunity to reflect and meditate on Pierre-Auguste Renoir's *A Girl with a Watering Can*.

As I stood in front of the painting, I began to notice Renoir's use of light and color. My memory flashed back to our Faith and Existence class, where we'd discussed the rise of romanticism and the eventual emergence of impressionism and its impact on our journey of faith. I had read Plato's *Republic* and reflected on his observation that beauty is the only spiritual essence we love instinctively by our nature, and we should use it as an avenue to the Transcendent Good. Ideas of God filled my mind, which swelled with a sense of gratitude. In a series of snapshots across my twenty-five-year-old life, I thought about various ways God had been real and present to me and how I felt his goodness all around despite my own experience of grief and suffering due to Don's death two years earlier.

Gradually, my ecstasy and experiences of euphoria subsided. As they did, I noticed a lady standing nearby crying softly. A slow stream of tears gently creased her cheek as she fought to subdue her unexpected emotion. Not sure what to do, but moved by compassion, I reached out to her and asked if she would like to talk. She nodded quietly, and we moved to the coffee shop where we ordered and settled in for a forty-five-minute conversation.

I discovered that the painting reminded her of her seven-year-old daughter, who had died a year earlier from leukemia. As she spoke, I felt a deep sadness not only for her loss, but also for Don's widow and children who now lived every day with a similar, painful reality. Despite never having lost a child myself, I felt drawn into the common human experience of suffering because of this encounter.

Romans 12:15 implores us to weep with those who weep and rejoice with those who rejoice, learning to be emotionally present with other people. So often these chance encounters with complete strangers helps us gain insight into how God works by seeing God at work in another person's circumstances. These moments allow us to see the realities of life and how God comes alongside us in new ways.

BIBLICAL INSIGHT FOR MAKING A REDEMPTIVE RESPONSE

The Bible tells us we've been created in Christ Jesus for good works: "He who began a good work in you will bring it to completion" (Philippians 1:6). The word our Bibles translate as *completion* comes from *telos*, which means "to fulfill our God-given purpose and destiny." This requires us to seek the fullness of all God intends us to do and to be. How can we develop both a capacity to learn and a commitment to grow and make a redemptive response to natural disasters, terminal illness, and human evil?

We need to stay emotionally present. Paul urges us to "rejoice with those who rejoice and weep with those who weep" (Romans 12:15). We need to be present and attentive when we're with those who are suffering. Recent research in neuroscience discovered that human connection experienced through emotional presence provides one of the most reassuring realities for people. Feeling the touch of someone we love and know loves us offers an effective remedy for suffering-induced anxiety.[9]

We also need to put our experiences of suffering in a framework of meaning that makes sense. This enlarges our plausibility structure, or mental map, so we can respond with understanding. If our belief in God excludes the possibility of evil and suffering, we've failed to face the realities of life and the hard truths communicated through Scripture and Christian experience. Our thinking often becomes paralyzed by why two people can face the same reality, receive the same input, but make fundamentally different responses. Matthew 13 points out that some are ever hearing but never understanding, always seeing but never perceiving. In one of his many poignant fragments, Pascal writes that there is "enough light for those who want to see and enough darkness for those of a contrary disposition."[10]

We must see where our egocentrism gets appropriately checked as we face the reality of suffering. The Stoic philosopher Epictetus once asked rhetorically, "What is the outcome for those who refuse to learn from suffering? Their outcome is to remain as they are."[11] Often, we believe if we only have enough evidence we'll be able to believe or not believe. But the answer involves more than evidence. We need to ask what is reasonable to believe given both the strengths and limits of human reason.

Finally, we recognize how our life with God includes our adequate response to suffering so we can approach the fullness of life God created us for. I believe every one of us has a God-given purpose and that our deepest satisfaction comes when we find the context that maximizes our God-given gifts and abilities for the greater good.

I find it helpful to modify and expand the classic three-fold formulation of the spiritual life—preparation, illumination, and union—to a seven-fold articulation: preparation, illumination, insight, embracing the insight, learning a deeper reality about God, embracing a greater dependence on God, and uniting with God to fulfill his purposes for our life.

Throughout this chapter, we've considered the realities related to the crucible of human suffering. We've discussed viewing natural disasters as the way God created the physical universe with laws and patterns that operate without regard for human life. This understanding helps us look for meaning beyond this life. Then, we've considered how we can endure the suffering that sudden death and terminal illness cause. Our response to loss completes the event and helps us react redemptively.

FOR REFLECTION

1. During this chapter, we've considered suffering at the hands of nature, terminal illness, and human evil. What are your experiences of suffering?

2. Are there any experiences you have had that make you question the reality of an all-powerful, all-knowing, all-loving God?

3. How do you see God in the midst of your suffering?

4. How has suffering affected your life, both for good and for ill?

5. Have you been able to find a community of fellow sufferers from whom you gain acceptance and inherent understanding?

6. How are you different, and how are you living differently, as a result of your suffering and as a response to your suffering?

7

THE CRUCIBLE OF PERSONAL CHOICE

But if you do not do what is right, sin is crouching at your door; it desires to have you, but you must rule over it.

GOD TO CAIN, GENESIS 4:7 NIV

But the Hebrew word, the word "timshel"—thou mayest— that gives a choice. It might be the most important word in the world. That says the way is open.

LEE, COMMENTING ON GENESIS 4 IN *EAST OF EDEN*, JOHN STEINBECK

The thing that David had done displeased the LORD.

2 SAMUEL 11:27

TRAGEDY OCCASIONALLY OCCURS through neglect. At other times, it arises from institutionally imposed priorities. Often, it results from our own personal choices. David, considered the greatest king in the Old Testament, was also one of the most flawed personalities in the Bible. In response to the utter treachery of David's adultery with Bathsheba, and his duplicitous cover-up in ordering Uriah to the front lines so he'd be killed,

2 Samuel 11:27, simply notes "the thing that David had done displeased the LORD."

What a blunt, direct way to summarize this entire episode. David
had broken the moral order of the universe. The Bible describes the
various ways David chose to behave as creating complications in his
life he could have avoided. He faces leadership challenges, and his own
family comes apart. Despite being God's chosen leader and remembered as a man after God's own heart, David behaved in treacherous,
self-justifying ways that led to a lifetime of upheaval resulting from
his personal choices.

Less dramatically but equally importantly, we often struggle to
accept that many of the complicating factors in our own life result
from decisions we've made—or failed to make. We acquiesce to the
invitation of a wayward friend, we stay in a difficult and demeaning
relationship, or we neglect to act when circumstances change or we
face temptation. In each instance, our role in the event creates a
lasting and negative impact we find difficult to overcome.

In John Steinbeck's novel *East of Eden,* the story turns on an important conversation between three characters: Lee, a cook and house-
keeper; his employer, Adam, a central character in the novel; and
Samuel, a leader in the community. Lee has been conducting an in-
depth Bible study on the book of Genesis and especially the Hebrew
word *timshel.* He concludes that humans exercise a great deal more
influence over their destiny than they often realize. Later in the novel,
this idea reemerges when Adam's son Cal recognizes he's not destined
for a disastrous life but can choose a different path and overcome and
break the cycle of human evil that has been his family's legacy.
Steinbeck elevates the individual and recognizes the reality that our
decisions determine our destiny. We're free to choose the moral path
we wish to follow in life.

More recently, Meg Jay writes that many twenty-somethings think
that thirty is the new twenty and believe they can suspend their life

for ten years, check out, do whatever they want, and then check back in when they turn thirty. But she identifies, demonstrates, and amplifies that seven of the ten most important decisions we make in life occur—or we lay the groundwork for them—in our twenties.[1]

These concrete and literary examples reflect the way some of us underestimate the benefits of pursuing a new direction, overestimate the consequences, or lack a sense of risk. As we fluctuate between these competing realities, we often become paralyzed by indecision. Moreover, we're tempted to play the what-if game.

Daniel Kahneman writes poignantly about the natural human response of regret. It reflects our protective urge to imagine a single choice changing the destiny of our life in ways that seldom if ever happen.[2] In helping us understand decision-making, Kahneman explains how the preset dispositions in our personality influence our actions. Writing specifically about how various forms of representative and implicit biases develop, Kahneman helps us recognize that many of our decisions aren't clear-cut. We develop shortcuts that allow us to make complex decisions quickly, believing we see things as they are and don't need to engage in deeper reflection or deliberation. But Kahneman points out all the false dilemmas we create for ourselves when we rely on our intuition alone to guide our decision-making. Thinking fast (intuition) works when we're driving and changing lanes, but other decisions require that we "think slow" (deliberative reasoning) to make the right choice.

Years ago, the movie *Sophie's Choice*[3] (based on the book by William Styron) highlighted this reality in the tragic moral dilemma a mother faced as she and her two children were shipped off to concentration camps during World War II. Which child will live? While most of our decisions fail to be this dramatic or tragic, they still alter our life.

KIERKEGAARD'S EITHER/OR

Another helpful example comes from Soren Kierkegaard's classic, *Either/Or*, where he amplifies the fundamental importance of personal choices in shaping our life.[4] I first read his work in an undergraduate philosophy class, but his ideas took on meaning and importance during a pivotal course in seminary. We studied several of his key works, including this two-volume classic, where Kierkegaard expresses his belief that we must choose between living a life of endless diversion—the aesthetic life—or committing ourselves in specific ways that create a foundation and continuity to our life across time—the ethical life. He embodies his ideas in two contrasting personalities.

Aesthetes build their life on immediacy. They seek to gratify every passing whim and desire. They believe the goal of life is perpetual gratification and spend their days chasing one unique experience after another, never stopping to ask if their life will yield anything of enduring meaning and fulfillment. The "accidents" of beauty, natural ability, or inherited wealth provide the foundation for life. (By "accidents," Kierkegaard means the personal gifts and abilities we've been given that were never generated by ourselves.) They blame any sense of dissatisfaction on externals: "If only I had a better job," "If only my circumstances were different or better," and so on. Everything in life is defined by its ability to be interesting or entertaining or somehow more alluring.

But aesthetes lack a unifying thread or meaning to their life, which creates problems for them. They simply live with a perpetual lust for enjoyment and diversion. Ultimately, aesthetes demonstrate greater concern with changing their environment than with changing themselves.

Ethical people, by contrast, build their life on long-term commitments, embodied by a judge who commits to a forty-year marriage. Rather than seeking the accidents of money, good looks, power, or fame, they embrace the essential dignity and worth of the human spirit. Ethical people build their life on the choices they make, consistent with what they believe to be right or wrong. To act ethically is to act significantly. They pursue life-giving and life-sustaining purposes, recognizing that life holds more than a series of momentary experiences or a search for everything exciting and new. The ethical life offers thrills and excitements without being built on the quest for the unique and different.

Ultimately, the ethical person understands the purposes fundamental to human existence. What we share in common allows us to make choices and commitments that endure. Every one of us can commit ourselves to being honest and dependable. Choosing to live the ethical life establishes a foundation for building a meaningful life. It also provides the grounding and foundation we need to lead well.

NEUROSCIENCE, EMOTIONAL INTELLIGENCE, AND DECISION-MAKING

More recently, studies in neuroscience and decision-making have revealed the role emotion plays in helping us understand the multiple dimensions of our circumstances and how these factors shape our choices and affect our decision-making. Interest has exploded in the past thirty years in studying how all other aspects of our nervous system affect our brain. This insatiable need to know and understand has given rise to the field of emotional intelligence and the recognition that past distinctions between the brain and the body—once referred to as the mind-body dualism—falsely characterizes how we think and act.

As recently as 2007, groundbreaking research demonstrates how accidents that damage the prefrontal cortex fundamentally impair our ability to analyze, plan, and make moral decisions. These studies conclusively establish that brain trauma in distinct areas negatively affect the ability to make sound moral judgments. Antonio Damasio, the lead neuroscientist on the project, explained that injuries to the prefrontal cortex impede good judgments because brain trauma disrupts our ability to process information, including our intuitive assessment of a decision's emotional impact.[5]

In one telling case, a brilliant lawyer with an IQ of 160 suffered head trauma to the prefrontal cortex in a major car accident. Although the attorney survived, the long road to recovery required intense efforts to recover the capacity to make sound personal and professional judgments. His inability to do this baffled the researchers as the attorney's IQ remained intact. They realized eventually that discerning the weight and gravity of various factors in decision-making depended on the engagement of key areas in the prefrontal cortex. In other words, individuals depend on this region of the brain to provide and regulate emotional input to make sound judgments or decisions.

Researchers then determined that the prefrontal cortex also manages complex social interactions typical of human communities. The attorney with the high IQ but damaged prefrontal cortex continued to understand highly complex principles, but every aspect of his relational life fell apart: his marriage ended, his business deteriorated, and he frequently behaved erratically in public.

Similar studies conducted at other institutions also examined what caused a variety of disrupting experiences, including "emotional flooding."[6] For example, researchers sought to understand and predict "amygdala hijacks," which occur in the part of our brain regulating our flight-or-fight response when we're under duress.[7] Recognizing what triggers these hijacks, when emotion takes over, provides crucial and significant information for anyone in leadership. Key causes include experiencing disrespect and complete disorientation.

IMPLICATIONS OF EMOTIONAL INTELLIGENCE FOR OUR LEADERSHIP

An example from my professional life explains how this affects us. I worked with an individual who struggled to get along with his board of directors. Through a variety of deteriorating experiences and exchanges, this individual completely lost composure and reacted to an instance of disrespect in a counterproductive way that ultimately altered and limited his career: he got fired.

In the aftermath of this event and because I was involved in this individual's life as a professional mentor, I did a great deal of soul-searching to understand why I failed to anticipate this implosion that occurred; I discovered the world of neuroscience research. The emerging field of emotional intelligence provided great insight and I continue to be interested in it. Last summer, I completed a series of seminars on the role of neuroscience in leadership. But twenty-five years ago, I struggled to understand why this individual had self-destructed. Eventually, I saw that we need to develop our ability to self-regulate, but we rarely engage in the kind of disciplines that lead to self-awareness and self-correction. The pattern of overreacting to experiences of disrespect became the norm and not the exception in this individual's life. Learning that disrespect was the single most significant cause of amygdala hijacks helped me understand what had occurred in this specific situation.

I'm captivated by the emerging field of emotional intelligence based on neuroscience research, particularly as it pertains to the specific and significant role it plays in the decisions and choices we make. Deeper insight into how these new discoveries can shape and affect our life helps us become better leaders.

Daniel Goleman's seminal work on emotional intelligence is pivotal.[8] He separates it into five core areas: self-awareness, self-regulation, empathy, social awareness, and social skills and engagement. Eventually, he consolidated the overarching categories but kept the same twenty-five specific areas illustrating emotional intelligence.

Starting with *self-awareness*, Goleman emphasizes that all emotional intelligence begins with our ability to be aware of and understand our own thoughts, feelings, and motivations. This takes time and dedicated reflection through prayer. I've found that starting every morning with a basic structure of reading Scripture, reading a key piece of literature, and praying and meditating on what happened the day before and what lies ahead has helped me develop a better capacity to understand my motives and behaviors. Often, I find myself reflecting on interpersonal interactions that led to a spectrum of outcomes. Why did some succeed and why did others not go as well or even turn out poorly? What was my role in the situation and circumstance?

Then, with *self-regulation* we demonstrate a comfort level with ambiguity and change by showing that we can control our impulses through integrity of purpose and continuity of character over time. In other words, we show ourselves to be consistent, dependable, and predictable, essential qualities of effective leadership. Over time, I've become more aware of how my response in the moment either lingers in the situation and causes further disruption, or quickly resolves it and helps the individuals and our response to events move forward. Recognizing the role we play in every situation, including how we maintain composure with our attitude and engagement, can help us initiate plans and respond constructively to changes, which keeps programs, projects, and people on track.

Third, *empathy* demonstrates our capacity to understand circumstances from another person's point of view, by developing a capacity to find common ground with people from all walks of life. Throughout my adult life and career, I've benefited enormously from the presence of key mentors. They've been more than executive coaches or consultants; they've helped me explore issues and challenges I face to gain perspective on my situation. I've also discovered that individuals open to mentors typically manifest a teachable spirit and a willingness to learn, both from their successes and especially from their setbacks. As a result, our capacity to receive mentoring and respond positively to coaching also equips us to cultivate empathy and act compassionately.

The ability to focus on others serves as an especially important hallmark of *social awareness* and leads to effective leadership through the cultivated skill to get work done through others. But you have to understand how your requests, plans, and execution of strategies play out both with your direct reports and throughout the entire organization.

Peter Drucker once said you have to disappoint people at a rate they can endure. I have found this to be an important gauge of workplace morale that influences the energy and commitment to new initiatives and future plans. People need to have enough confidence in the value of what they're being asked to do—and that it will contribute to a greater good than they're already experiencing. Otherwise, the nerve of human motivation gets bruised or even cut, damaging or destroying the decision to participate with our best energies.

Finally, develop *social skills* that build rapport with people both similar to and different from yourself. Drucker also said good manners act as the social lubrication of every effective organization. That's a classy way to say treat others the way you want them to treat you. Give your coworkers the benefit of the doubt. Even when they let you down, figure out ways to stay emotionally present so you can continue to engage them in ways that produce positive outcomes.

These five elements of emotional intelligence require a strong self-motivation to perform, as well as a capacity to develop a vision and motivate others to pursue it. Vision-casting requires a desire for and capacity to develop a relational network both instrumental and essential to our success. Ultimately, an effective leader must demonstrate the cognitive capacities to combine big-picture thinking with attention to the details and plans that lead to implementing a strategic vision successfully.

As I delved more deeply into each of these areas, I experienced the process of brain mapping. Although the reliability of results from this area of research continues to be debated, I remain intrigued by how the brain and the body interact in executive performance and personal choice. The nine areas of executive function essentially fall into three core divisions: focus endurance (enduring and maintaining focus), neuro-strength (paying attention to the right things), and focus capacity (controlling impulses to overcome distractions). They all interact to influence the choices we ultimately make.

Emotional intelligence and the exploding field of neuroscience help us understand the role various areas of our brain play in our emotional and intellectual makeup and how they interact as we make decisions that influence and guide our life. One region, the anterior cingulate, plays a critical role in governing our emotions and feelings in relationship to our reason and logic. Here we develop a capacity to regulate our emotional response to external circumstances. Additionally, through this interaction, we begin to assess the intentions and emotional states of others to analyze our external situation and determine an appropriate response.

The anterior cingulate, part of the prefrontal cortex, carries out essential activities so that we can develop an accurate capacity to sense what others are thinking and feeling. It influences us in at least seven key areas: solving problems, managing impulses, expressing feelings, relating to others, processing social cues, responding intuitively, and experiencing empathy.

Equally significant, the amygdala determines our fight-or-flight response, activated when we experience stress or trauma or perceive that we're under threat. The amygdala's biggest drawback is registering fear or anxiety when we encounter behavior we perceive to be adverse. Five perceptions or experiences can trigger the flight-or-fight response: condescension, lack of respect, unfair treatment, perceptions of being unappreciated and ignored, or being held to unrealistic deadlines. The outward expression of these inward states often leads to counterproductive and career-limiting behavior, including manifestations of anger, fear, and other impulsive, self-destructive behaviors.

Fortunately, we can learn to overcome these responses. Andrew Newberg, who once taught at University of Pennsylvania and now serves on the faculty at Baylor University, has done significant and consequential work on how we can develop certain regions of the brain for greater emotional intelligence and self-control. He and his colleagues determined that twelve minutes a day of prayer and meditation could fundamentally rewire the brain for greater self-regulation and control.[9] Specifically, this activity strengthens the anterior cingulate and helps us become more aware of others and attentive to how they perceive our emotional state and potential response. (For comparative analysis, I encourage you to review step four in the twelve-step recovery movement process. The vigorous moral inventory of step four is synonymous with the moral inventory advocated by the fourth-century monk Evagrius and embodied today by the popularity of the Enneagram.)

This finding assists us in understanding the relevance of ancient spirituality and the value of synchronizing the table of virtues and vices Evagrius of Pontus crafted in the fourth century. Moving effort-lessly between this monk's taxonomy of virtues and vices with their modern equivalents is illuminating. The failings of chronic overwork, road rage, consumption, schadenfreude (envy that seeks to destroy another), narcissism, unbridled desire, midlife crisis, and depression born of despair are modern equivalents of ancient vices afflicting the human soul. Through prayer and meditation, we can develop alter-native neuro paths for our desires and how to satisfy them.

Ultimately, these studies and practices help us understand the con-nections between emotion, social functioning, and personal decision-making. Growing evidence suggests that the brain functions essential for learning—attention, memory activation, decision-making, and social functioning—are all profoundly influenced by both our cog-nitive and emotional registries. This relationship helps us commit to causes greater than ourselves that will outlive us, the manifestation of a desire to choose a particular path that leads to an enduring life of significance and impact.

CHOOSING TO LEARN: EXPERIENCE-BASED LEADERSHIP DEVELOPMENT

A growing body of literature focuses on experience-based learning and how organizations and whole industries are creating a culture of con-tinuous improvement.[10] Studies that demonstrate the importance of ten thousand hours of applied learning to develop expertise have been pivotal. But time on the job doesn't guarantee expertise. You need the right experiences combined with the right guidance. Otherwise, you "have the experience, but miss the meaning." What pivotal experiences with proper guidance lead to effective leadership? How can we avoid the career-limiting mistakes that cause total career derailment? Scholars identify at least seven experiences.[11]

First, learn to be open-minded and flexible in thought and action. In other words, cultivate a disposition to look at each situation and figure out what will work best without always imposing a preset formula as a solution to every action. We can create routines, but we need to recognize that appropriate responses to situations vary.

Second, develop a curiosity about others that manifests in cultural sensitivity and interest. We often think this only applies in a global context. In reality, every organization, like every society, possesses a unique culture. We need to understand and pay attention to both key similarities and differences.

Third, develop the ability to separate the mundane from the highly irregular and complex—and understand how to respond appropriately to each. This calls for good judgment based on learning to balance competing commitments, an ability we develop with time, experience, and committed mentors. Drucker always emphasized that we should never work for somebody who only focuses on our weaknesses. Instead, work for people who focus on our strengths and will hire to cover our weaknesses so they're irrelevant. In the process, we get the opportunity to make decisions and execute plans that lead to a lot of success but also some predictable failures. How we respond to failure will determine our destiny. Can we recover from a series of singular mistakes and learn how to grow from them going forward? Or do they fundamentally destroy us?

Fourth, be resilient, resourceful, optimistic, and energetic. My focus throughout this entire book is on being resilient and resourceful.

I've learned that effective leadership must combine a posture of optimism with a dynamism of stamina and significant energy.

Fifth, it's essential for us to cultivate fundamental honesty and integrity. Religious and secular organizations alike rely on the basic expectation of human integrity. Otherwise, we have no way to build sustainable organizations or meaningful lives and careers.

Sixth, do everything in our power to build a stable personal life. This finding, which comes from a completely multicultural, human-centered perspective, reveals that those with a stable personal life have more intellectual and emotional resources available for their work.

Finally, develop baseline competencies that inspire the confidence of peers and associates. Some technical and leadership capacities must begin at a basic level of expertise to inspire confidence in our strategies, plans, and objectives. We can't ignore this factor—but equally important, we can't let it overrun us.

BIBLICAL INSIGHT FROM JOSHUA'S CHOICE

Joshua said to the children of Israel: "Choose this day whom you will serve, whether the gods your fathers served in the region beyond the River, or the gods of the Amorites in whose land you dwell. But as for me and my house, we will serve the LORD" (Joshua 24:15).

Joshua reminds us that our ultimate decision is choosing to align our life and destiny with God. As his life and leadership was nearing its end, he articulated one of the most profound farewell speeches in the entire landscape of Scripture. "Choose this day whom you will serve" anchored the memory and imagination of the children of Israel to the responsibility they carried for their future. Joshua identified the opportunities and the temptations that lie ahead: the children of Israel could follow earlier or current examples, or they could attach their destiny to the rich, vibrant, pulsating life with God that animates the entire story of Scripture. What is amazing is this same opportunity is given to us: Will we follow past patterns and establish ruts, or engage the rich adventure that comes from living our life with God? The choice we make will shape our entire life journey.

FOR REFLECTION

From ancient texts to modern novels, our literature and experiences teach us that our choices matter. They make a difference in the contour of our life. They provide enormous joy and can also be the source of debilitating pain.

Centuries ago, Saint Augustine wrote *The City of God*, his magnum opus outlining the way God's presence in Roman society had ebbed and flowed with the rise of the early church and throughout the empire's one-thousand year history. According to Augustine, rather than causing the demise of the Roman Empire, the Christian church preserved the civilization long after it should have collapsed. Building on this theme of choices, he demonstrated that all human history reflects a choice between aligning our life with the will of God or being self-willed—and between choosing to live our life with a love for God or being full of self-love. Two wills and two loves.

More recently, leaders and scholars alike have focused on the need to make key choices based on core competencies that lead to predictable outcomes. Here are six areas in which we make choices by answering questions that shape our life and our ultimate contribution.

Choice 1. In what way or ways do you demonstrate respect for cultures different from your own rather than elevating and esteeming your culture above all others?

Choice 2. How well do you understand your business—its strategies, appropriate structure, organizational processes, and specialized knowledge?

Choice 3. How do you successfully and effectively lead and manage others in the selection, development, motivation, team competency, and capacity of your employees? When necessary, how do you terminate key members of your leadership team and organization?

Choice 4. How do you stay attentive to your organizational culture while attending to pressures that come from your wider social, political, and industry context?

Choice 5. On a scale of one to five, with one being least effective and five being most effective, rate yourself in the following areas of qualities and competencies of an effective leader.

- Listens carefully and asks helpful questions.

- Works to see the world through other people's point of view.

- Is open and honest.

- Has a reputation of being fair.

- Balances an appropriate level of being predictable and flexible as needed.

- Is adaptable when circumstances require an alternative direction or approach.

- Is willing to embrace strategic risks.

- Perseveres to work through surprises and setbacks.

- Is optimistic, accepts responsibility for outcomes, and works to learn from and correct obvious mistakes.

- Is able to manage their own affairs without unnecessary distraction or disruption.

What step would you like to take to grow in just one of these areas?

Choice 6. What choices do you make that show your allegiance to a God-shaped love and life? Where are you not sure? Where have you failed to make these choices either by omission or commission?

Recognizing that we have a tremendous opportunity and responsibility as we make choices that shape our destiny can be simultaneously exhilarating and terrifying. Like Saint Augustine, and Joshua before him, we can decide to align our life and love with the life and love of God—and that will make all the difference.

CONCLUSION

WISDOM FOR THE JOURNEY

*David, after he had served the purpose of God in his own
generation, fell asleep and was laid with his fathers*

ACTS 13:36

*An effective leader is not somebody who wakes up in the morning and
asks, 'What do I want to do?' Instead, an effective leader is someone
who wakes up every morning and asks, "What needs to get done?"*

PETER DRUCKER

WE MADE IT!" This cryptic message from Ernest Shackleton
to his wife back in England told her he'd survived in Ant-
arctica. It also sums up what it feels like to endure a season of crucibles
and come out on the other side. The crucibles persist, and their refining fire continues to shape and challenge us, but we can pause and
look back over this extended period of time and see growth and change.

Nancy Koehn highlights the important responsibility of paying attention to our shifting circumstances so we can understand and innovate in meaningful and successful ways when difficulties arise from
uncharted circumstances.[1] Likewise, David Brooks, in *The Second
Mountain*, speaks about the ways we can respond to the crucibles that
shape us.[2] His timely wisdom helps guide us as we strive to move
beyond the dichotomy of the resumé virtues and the eulogy virtues to

embrace the meaning and joy of committing ourselves to purposes that will outlive us. His unique contribution lies in encouraging us to make and keep four enduring commitments: "to a vocation, to a spouse and family, to a philosophy or faith, and to a community."[3] These commitments fundamentally refine us into the kind of people who can discover and live the good life despite any setback or circumstance.

The question of the good life first arose in the pre-Christian era when the Greeks and Romans wondered: What is the good life? Who is a good person? How do I become the kind of person who can find and fulfill this longing for the good life? And, as I pursue this life, how do I make sense of suffering, and how do I reconcile the idea of a loving God with it?

Every one of us must answer these enduring questions. We never face the same exact circumstances, but we confront the same exact challenges. The long and storied history of these questions and our response to them winds through the important figure of Saint Augustine. In *The City of God*, Augustine helps us recognize that all human history involves the unfolding drama of two loves and two wills.[4] We're people guided either by self-love or by the love of God, and we choose to be self-willed or we align our will with the will of God.

This insight continues to be true today. As our society careens through the vicissitudes of our cultural moment, Robert Putnam's work *The Upswing* identifies six essential elements shaping our modern mentality: economic inequality, political polarization, social isolation, cultural narcissism, racial conflict, and gender inequality.

This framework of analysis promotes understanding. Despite the ongoing and emerging challenges, learning to persevere in the face of trial brings tremendous insight that refines our response. All of these resources combine to provide both insight and strategy, but we have to learn how to look and see, to hear and understand.

A central part of our life with God is learning how to connect the discrete experiences of our individual life with wider narratives of meaning and purpose. Many, if not all, of us struggle to see a pattern to our life or understand the purpose behind our individual experiences. We walk most of our lives in the dark, without attaining nearly as much understanding as we would like, even when we occasionally catch a glimpse of God's grand design.

Beyond our personal experiences lie our corporate responsibilities. We have to wake up every morning and ask not what do we want to do, but what needs to get done. This book testifies to what can happen when the vision we're trying to accomplish exceeds the inconvenience of setback and challenge. This is what it means to persevere. These crucible moments can stretch into years, and the energy required can seem both unending and exhausting. But we also experience breakthrough moments when we move beyond the crucibles and find new meaning and purpose in our life and work.

I started the book with the crucible of missed meaning, because it represents an effort to identify and elevate the way we overlook so many experiences of our everyday life. We literally miss the meaning and consequently the opportunity for deeper understanding and a better response. We can broaden our impact and enjoyment of life by recognizing the importance of mentors, educational programs, and guided experience. One personal example is the way the multiple degrees I've pursued have profoundly changed me. I remember experiencing the intensity of studying for my qualifying exams and writing my dissertation; it felt like my brain was changing as I worked around the clock to gain mastery of an area of human knowledge. Likewise, I vividly recall the first day of my first class with Peter Drucker. He said, "Many of you are here because you believe the mission of your organization is the most important thing in the world. But I'm here to help you understand that if you don't manage your money, you won't get to do your mission." In an instant, my entire perception shifted to recognizing that we need to share a love of ideas with a love of well-run organizations to lead well.

The second crucible, the crucible of enduring challenge, elevates the importance of persevering and helps us see that *effective* leadership often means *enduring* leadership. To persevere and not be sidelined or destroyed by our challenges requires a combination of grit and self-regulation. Nothing replaces getting through hardship. Every one of us goes through it. Some of us make it out the other side, but all of us face setbacks and challenges that become proving grounds for our character.

Of course, many elements of our life remain completely outside of our control. The crucible of human treachery discusses this particularly painful yet enduring reality that undermines our effectiveness, damages esprit de corps, and causes immediate and long-term harm to our organization. I include this crucible because it's so pervasive in both modern society and human history, and it always has the same effect: destroying trust and undermining the sense of purpose we derive from doing meaningful work with meaningful people. We must go beyond identifying this treachery as an abstract reality to honoring public and personal agreements for integrity to endure.

But trust is always a two-way street. It's one thing to refrain from recounting the whole event. It's quite another to create a false narrative, either by shading information or creating an entirely untruthful account. But control what you can control, what you say, and how you say it. You can control whether or not you represent situations accurately or not, even if you're unable to share everything. Claiming to be transparent and being transparent are two different things. If being transparent means sharing sensitive information in a non-legal context, it's not appropriate or allowed. Ultimately, we'll encounter people who claim one thing while representing another. Our greatest responsibility in these moments is resisting the temptation to retaliate. Instead, we must rise above the circumstance.

Our cultural moment has elevated the long "arc of the moral universe . . . [that] bends toward justice" and the importance of the crucible of awakened moral conscience. Eventually, this crucible comes to all of us. Sometimes, because of hardship, it occurs early in life. At other, more predictable times, it comes to us through expanded social and cultural experiences and responsibilities. Regardless of the timing, it always changes us by expanding our perception and helping us see and understand the nature of our life and the context in which we live it.

Martin Luther King Jr.'s life illustrates how individuals can experience the awakening of moral conscience—if they'll allow it. He believed in the love of God but also saw into the abyss of human nature. Never losing his confidence in the ultimate power of love to win out over hate, King nonetheless faced a series of incomplete victories, including a season of challenge and setback. Yet he never lost heart. He stayed physically and emotionally present to the movement and its ideals and worked tirelessly to craft strategies that would bring God's healing and redemptive power to our country and our world. He provides such a heartening and encouraging example despite the ugly reality of hatred and bigotry.

The fifth crucible, the crucible of social conflict, helps us understand and respond to long-simmering tensions throughout our country. Festering realities arising from unfulfilled promises often set social conflicts in motion. We recognize that we need to make real and constructive efforts to address social issues that plague us. The life and legacy of John Lewis has reminded us of the epic journey so many embarked on in the last seventy years. Jon Meacham, in his book *His Truth Is Marching On*, writes beautifully of the essence of Lewis's remarkable life by elevating his deeply held convictions that nonviolent, civil disobedience was "not only a biblical imperative but a transforming reality."[5]

This commitment gave Lewis the spiritual strength to endure personal hardship and corporate setback as he pursued the greater good of a free and equitable society. He reminds us how to balance bedrock convictions about what should be done with the steadfast energy to persevere despite the reluctance or even resistance of others to join the wider movement.

The sixth crucible, the crucible of human suffering, represents where I have lived so much of my time at Westmont. The problem of evil and suffering that comes to us through natural disaster, life-destroying disease, and human evil can feel unfair and unrelenting. The experience of natural disaster seems to suggest that the laws of nature and of nature's God operate with little to no regard for human life and our grand purposes to build human communities. In each of these events, we experienced a real and present threat to our campus, our sense of purpose as a college, and even our entire community.

Life-destroying disease and evil at the hands of other humans also threaten us. I experienced the grief and suffering that occurs when loved ones die early or out of sequence as a result of cancer, heart disease, or accidents during surgery. In every case, these experiences have presented opportunities to respond in life-affirming or life-altering ways. In fact, every experience of disease-related death has followed the pattern of suffering and grief captured in the Psalms of lament. These passages respond to suffering and loss in a way that allows us not only to cry out in protest and anguish to God, but to rely and lean on him as we work our way through our suffering.

But beyond suffering because of nature, disease, and accidental death, anguish resulting from human evil remains the most opaque and mysterious. It's impossible to penetrate the veil of a human personality motivated by evil. Despite the explanations and the efforts to make rational sense of irrational behavior, human evil eludes any complete or total explanation. Its presence seems to violate the basic laws of human nature. Yet it endures in its most grotesque form as senseless bombings of civilian populations or capital crimes committed against complete strangers. We simply have no complete way to explain or understand the motives behind such behavior. For those of us in harm's way, this reality requires that we learn to find meaning even in the most meaning-destroying circumstances.

Finally, as part of our growth and maturity as humans, we must embrace those times when we face crucibles completely or largely of our own making. Clearly, we sometimes just make mistakes. At other times, plans simply fail to work out. Occasionally, we make choices that end up going terribly wrong. In the crucible of personal choice, we confront acts of omission and acts of commission that undermine our impact and curb our effectiveness. In circumstances like these, we're tempted to play the what-if game and create scenarios in which one altered decision leads to a completely different and positive outcome. But life is seldom, if ever, that easy. The work of Daniel Kahneman has helped me tremendously, especially his insight into the natural human response of regret. It illuminates the protective urge of humans to imagine we have more control over our circumstances than we actually do—while at the same time acknowledging we often play a role in the circumstances we face.

Ultimately, I have come to realize that the crucibles we face are woven into the fabric of life. This is what it means to be human: not to live a life free of trial, but to grow morally by learning how to respond to life's crucibles in ways that are redemptive, meaningful, and life-giving. We recognize that we can only do this if we're prepared to cultivate deeper self-awareness and a willingness to self-correct. We also need clarity of purpose and a vision of our life that draws us beyond hardships to see and realize their greater meaning. Vision always exceeds inconvenience. Vision always exceeds current capacity and resource, forcing us forward to invent new solutions to enduring problems. Eventually, we develop the strategies that engage our life energies in meaningful projects that will outlive us.

As a result of these crucibles, my own purpose in life continues to be refined. I find it incredibly meaningful to have projects and purposes that contribute to my personal sense of human flourishing as I work with and for people I love, know, and respect. Together these realities have allowed me to create a context and a culture to respond constructively to my crucibles while developing the resources to rise above them. And for this, I'm incredibly grateful.

ACKNOWLEDGMENTS

I WANT TO THANK THE MANY PEOPLE who encouraged me to write this book. The ideas presented here germinated in one of our earliest post-pandemic gatherings of college presidents. Then I brought these ideas into our own Westmont community, and some of the unique challenges we faced galvanized my own thinking about the crucibles that shape us. Along the way, several distinct voices became important conversation partners, and I'd like to thank them now.

First and foremost, thanks to Cindy Bunch, vice president and associate publisher for InterVarsity Press, who has been fantastic throughout, guiding this project to its completion.

Then, Gregg Prickett, my Proverbs 18:24 friend, who has encouraged me throughout much of my adult life and especially during some of life's most challenging crucibles.

Nancy Phinney, although winding down her long and illustrious career at Westmont, has been indispensable throughout this entire project. She is an alum who has dedicated her life energy to telling the Westmont story far and wide. She still edits and proofreads everything I write, and more than anyone with whom I've ever worked, hears my voice as she edits.

Addie Smith, my executive assistant, has been invaluable as she has balanced the multiple demands on my time and our office while also embracing the many nuances of this project with great enthusiasm.

We would not have hit any of the deadlines along the way without her able assistance. Thanks, Addie.

My board of trustees has been especially important and remarkable during this time of great challenge. As the world forced everyone to work remotely, our board came closer to preserve and advance the mission of the college in critically important ways. This has been a long season of multiple shifts in strategies and tactics while learning how to lean on one another in new ways. I want to thank them by name: Mike Allen, Holly Anderson, Mary Barbour, Teri Bradford-Rouse, Phil Dunkelberger, Rick Fogg, Dave Gehring, Roy Goble, Marcus "Goodie" Goodloe, Ramon Gupta, Helga Houston, Denise Jackson, Tremper Longman, Patty Martin, Todd Mattson, Bob Nicholson, Roxanne Packham, Jim Richardson, Karen Robilio, Sharon Rose, Lynne Tahmisian, Mitch Vance, and Celeste White. As well as some who were with us and have recently retired from the board: Carol Houston, Ed Birch, Gary Harris, Vince Nelson, Tom Nelson, Steve Stong, and Mark Zoradi.

Thanks to my executive team. They are simply the best in the business and great friends and colleagues. Doug Jones, our vice president for finance and CFO, has been with me since August 2000; we're in our twenty-fourth year of working together. Doug is a great processing partner, a wonderful strategist, and is absolutely willing to work as long as it takes to engineer new solutions to vexing problems. He has been at the ground floor of everything we've done. He lives and works with the rare combination of humble confidence and intensity of will serving purposes greater than himself. Reed Sheard, our vice president for advancement and CIO, has been with me more than twenty years, and, like Doug, is a great member of the team with a wonderful creative mind and a willingness to pivot on a moment's notice to solve new problems in new ways. I always feel comfortable with him and am grateful for the multiple ways he serves the purposes of the college with creative and effective results. Edee Schulze, our vice president for student life, has been with me ten years, and I'm delighted she chose to join us in 2014. Edee has the amazing ability to deal with the day-to-day without taking her eye off the long-term objective of developing the whole person. She has made multiple pivots throughout the pandemic while serving on the frontlines with our students and their families. She is also one of the best integrators of multiple resources while crafting cutting-edge strategies. Irene Neller, our vice president for enrollment, marketing, and communication, joined the team December 1, 2017, just three days before the Thomas Fire erupted. By her second week on the job, we had moved to our Westmont Downtown campus after the county sheriff evacuated the campus. She has just been fantastic at developing strategies and communicating tactics to keep us close to our prospective students and their families. The boutique-style approach we've embraced resulted from Irene's dogged determination to let individuals experience our campus as they made their college decision. She has also taken our college communication to a level of excellence, garnering national and international attention. Finally, Kim Denu, our provost and chief academic officer, began at Westmont with the 2022–2023 academic year. Her wonderful, settled presence has brought fresh air to her work as we open up a whole new array of opportunities post-pandemic.

Rick Ifland, class of '83, who became a dear friend and colleague after we first met during my candidacy in the spring of 2007, and has served in so many roles at Westmont.

My extended family, but especially my siblings, Rich, Terry, and Londa, who make up the rich tapestry of our family of origin, and "Uncle Charlie" Nipp who has always taken a unique and meaningful interest in me and whose love of life and encouragement of others is infectious.

Our immediate family. I fundamentally believe we'll always find hidden blessings and silver linings if we look for them. One benefit of the pandemic was going home every day to eat lunch. Living on campus, as we do, meant I could work in my office every day. It also meant that we had long periods of uninterrupted time together that were special and memorable. During this period, all three of our children faced so many of life's most significant challenges while finding their significant others. So to Anna and Jared, Liz and Jack, and Ricky and Bayli, I say both congratulations and thank you. Each in your own way has inspired and blessed me.

Finally, I'm grateful for my wife, Pam, who always prefers being out of the limelight. It has been an amazing period on so many fronts, both personal and professional. For the things we can share with others, what an incredible period of growth and learning. For what will always remain private, thank you. Thank you for your endurance, your optimism, your joy, your patience, your compassion, your understanding, and for always carrying with me a vision for our work together that exceeds the inconvenience.

So many others have played a role in the stories and insights shared in this book. The faculty, staff, and administrators at Westmont, our key donors and friends, the vast network of Westmont alums, the greater Santa Barbara community, and so many more. I only wish I could take the time to thank you personally by name. Please accept my thanks now.

QUESTIONS FOR REFLECTION AND DISCUSSION

THIS GUIDE IS DESIGNED FOR GROUP DISCUSSION. You can select fifteen or so questions for a robust single session or break it into several sessions according to the needs of your group.

FOREWORD

David Brooks writes that intuition is a kind of knowledge held unconsciously but built up consciously by reading, observing, and reflecting.

1. What are the disciplines and activities that you utilize to understand your circumstances and craft your life response?

   a. In other words, what is your practice of reading?

   b. How often and in what ways do you reflect?

   c. How do you keep track of your observations and intuitions?

2. Are there any other personal practices and disciplines you've found helpful?

INTRODUCTION: LESSONS IN ENDURANCE

In the introduction, we read, "Crucibles bring suffering but they also offer transformative opportunities that shape our character and help us become the best version of ourselves."

1. Identify an experience of suffering and reflect on these three formative questions:

    a. What happened to you?

    b. What happened inside of you?

    c. What happened because of your experience of suffering, and your effort to understand it and to let it be a guiding insight in your life?

ONE: THE CRUCIBLE OF MISSED MEANING

1. Reflect on T. S. Eliot's observation, "They had the experience but they missed the meaning." What are a few examples from your own life when this has occurred?

2. Read Matthew 13:1-23, "The Parable of the Sower." The parables of Jesus are meant to teach us how to look with loving attention on other people, gain insight on our own life realities, see what's at play, and make a moral response. This happens because of our capacity for gestalt-type perceptual re-orientations where the realities before us don't shift but our perception of those realities does.

    a. What is something you are stuck on?

    b. Is there anything you've learned or haven't considered previously that would change or enlarge your understanding of your situation, even if nothing about the circumstance or situation changes?

TWO: THE CRUCIBLE OF ENDURING CHALLENGE

1. Read the "Twelve Enduring Lessons" list out loud. Which one(s) come easily, which one(s) are somewhat challenging, and which one(s) are real weak spots for you?

2. What do you think of Winston Churchill? Now that you've indicated your bias toward or against him, set that aside, and

critique where you think his life and leadership can help us and where it might limit us.

3. Frederick Douglass worked strategically to become a key talking partner with President Lincoln. Each of us has to weigh the impact of our life and contribution. What do you need to do differently to have the widest, most profound impact possible?

4. In writing about Henry Kissinger, I amplify certain key values and traits, including the necessity of intellectual curiosity and the importance of religious and moral values. From your own reading and reflection, what do you find most provocative in Kissinger's thoughts? What do you find least compelling?

5. How often do you take time to thank other people for something they've done or something they've said that encouraged you? How has your own practice of gratitude made your life better and fundamentally improved the lives of those around you?

THREE: THE CRUCIBLE OF HUMAN TREACHERY

1. Identify one or two experiences of human treachery when you've been the victim (only those you're comfortable sharing). Identify one or two experiences of human treachery where you were the cause. Did you respond like Judas or like Peter?

2. What, in your observation and experience, are the destructive impacts of human treachery? Are there noticeable steps, stages, or signals along the way that if confronted would have prevented the act(s) of treachery from occurring?

3. What strikes you about Dr. Friedman's "Family Systems" approach to organizational assessment, including the role of saboteurs and charlatans in highly reactive systems? What is your understanding of the Judas Syndrome and how can you counteract it, both personally and professionally?

4. Do the five causes of human treachery resonate with your own experience?

5. Do you struggle with or have you been the target of envy, either regular envy or schadenfreude?

FOUR: THE CRUCIBLE OF AWAKENED MORAL CONSCIENCE

1. Martin Luther King Jr. said, "If you haven't found something for which you're willing to die, you're not fit to live." Have you had a moral awakening that helps you know that for which you're willing to die in order that you'll be fit to live?

2. Several guiding realities that shaped the life and legacy of Dr. King are identified throughout this chapter. Which one(s) have impacted you? What additional one(s) are unique to you?

3. What role have key mentors, close friends, and transformative educational experiences played on your life?

4. Name one or two leaders of national and global movements today that you admire, and why?

FIVE: THE CRUCIBLE OF SOCIAL CONFLICT

1. What is your response to the following quote from John Lewis? "At a very early stage of the movement, I accepted the teaching of Jesus, the way of love, the way of nonviolence, the spirit of forgiveness and reconciliation. The idea that hate is too heavy a burden to bear. I don't want to go down that road. I've seen too much hate, seen too much violence. And I know love is a better way."

2. Do you have personal experiences that help galvanize your determination, including your determination to change the course of history?

3. I have found various individuals and writings helpful in crafting a constructive response to current social conflicts (including the idea of a "mutual accountability" approach). Identify and articulate various resources you have found as you have worked to make a constructive response to some dilemma or social situation that needs help.

4. In chapter five, an overview of Putnam and Romney's work, *The Upswing*, is provided. Together, they identify four major themes that have dominated the cultural milieu of America over the last 125 years: economic inequality, political polarization, social isolation, and cultural narcissism. How do you respond to their critique? Where is it inaccurate? Are there other forces at play that seem similarly or even more influential?

5. How can you take the example of John Lewis and others and gain motivation and inspiration for working to improve sectors of society that matter a great deal to you?

SIX: THE CRUCIBLE OF HUMAN SUFFERING

1. What are your experiences of evil and suffering? How do you understand them? What were their cause? What will be their lingering impact? Have you been able to identify ways in which your experiences and the work to understand them have helped you in your present life?

2. Simone Weil offers the beautiful analogy of how the sun is to the physical universe what God's love is to the spiritual universe. How do you experience the love of God in terms of making you a more loving, other-centered person?

3. What experiences have you had of natural disasters, sudden death, or terminal illness? How have you responded to them?

4. Elie Wiesel and Viktor Frankl write poignantly about the reality of human evil and especially its manifestation during the

Holocaust. In both cases, these men chose to make positive and redemptive responses by learning how to be emotionally present to the suffering of others. How have your own experiences of suffering impacted you, and have you been able to understand your own experiences well enough to be emotionally present to others?

SEVEN: THE CRUCIBLE OF PERSONAL CHOICE

1. Do you believe in the sovereignty of God?

2. Do you believe in human agency?

3. What role do you believe personal choice and human agency play in the sovereignty of God?

4. Recent discoveries in neuroscience and emotional intelligence have helped us understand the importance of self-regulation. What are your experiences of the benefits of self-regulation?

CONCLUSION: WISDOM FOR THE JOURNEY

1. After your life on earth is finished, how do you hope you're remembered? In other words, what purposes are you giving your life energy to that will outlive you?

NOTES

INTRODUCTION: LESSONS IN ENDURANCE

[1] Nancy Koehn, *Forged in Crisis: The Making of Five Courageous Leaders* (New York: Scribner Books, 2017).

[2] Friedrich Nietzsche, *Twilight of the Idols: How to Philosophize with a Hammer* (Oxford, UK: Oxford University Press, 1889), 6.

ONE: THE CRUCIBLE OF MISSED MEANING

[1] Iris Murdoch, *The Sovereignty of Good* (London, UK: Routledge, 2001), and various philosophical essays and novels.

[2] Charles Duhigg, *Smarter Faster Better: The Transformative Power of Real Productivity* (New York: Random House Trade Paperbacks, 2018), 71-102.

[3] Thomas Kuhn, *The Structure of Scientific Revolutions* (Chicago: The University of Chicago Press, 2012).

[4] Werner Jaeger, *Paideia: The Ideals of Greek Culture: Volume I, II, III* (Oxford, UK: Oxford University Press, 1934, 1947).

[5] *Places in the Heart*, directed by Robert Benton (Burbank, CA: TriStar Pictures, 1984).

[6] Erin Meyer, *The Culture Map: Breaking Through the Invisible Boundaries of Global Business* (New York: PublicAffairs Books, 2014), 29-34.

[7] Meyer, *The Culture Map*, 14-17.

[8] Daniel Kahneman, *Thinking, Fast and Slow* (New York: Farrar, Strauss and Giroux, 2011), 85-88.

[9] Kahneman, *Thinking, Fast and Slow*, 87.

[10] Gayle D. Beebe, *The Shaping of An Effective Leader: Eight Formative Principles of Leadership* (Downers Grove, IL: InterVarsity Press, 2011).

[11] Don Richardson, *Peace Child* (Ventura, CA: Regal Books, 1991).

[12] Saint Augustine, *Confessions* (New York: Penguin Books, 1961), 21.

TWO: THE CRUCIBLE OF ENDURING CHALLENGE

[1]Maili Tirel, "Why It's So Important to be Resilient: 3 Tips to Practice Resiliency," *Tracking Happiness*, January 2023, www.trackinghappiness.com/importance-of -resilience/.

[2]Tirel, "Why It's So Important to be Resilient." For an articulation of the GROW mindset, see scholars who codify these intuitions as: Good emotion, Reasonable expectations, Other-focused, and Wellness-motivated.

[3]Winston Churchill, *My Early Years: 1874–1904* (New York: Simon and Schuster, 1938, 1958, 1996).

[4]Andrew Roberts, *Churchill: Walking with Destiny* (New York and London: Penguin Random House, 2018).

[5]Candace Millard, *Hero of the Empire: The Boer War, a Daring Escape and the Making of Winston Churchill* (New York: Doubleday, 2016).

[6]Roy Jenkins, *Churchill: A Biography* (New York: Farrar, Straus and Giroux, 2001).

[7]Roberts, *Churchill: Walking with Destiny.*

[8]Erik Larson, *The Splendid and the Vile* (New York: Crown, 2020).

[9]Winston Churchill, *Great Contemporaries*, ed. James W. Muller (Wilmington, DE: ISI Press, 2012).

[10]Dominique Enright, *The Wicked Wit of Winston Churchill* (United Kingdom: Michael O'Mara Books, 2011), 22. Cita Stelzer, *Dinner with Churchill: Policy-Making at the Dinner Table* (New York: Pegasus Books, 2013).

[11]Winston Churchill, *Churchill: The Power of Words,* ed. Martin Gilbert (Philadelphia: Da Capo Press, 2012).

[12]Sonia Purnell, *Clementine* (New York: Penguin Random House, 2015).

[13]Morgan McCall Jr. and George P. Hollenbeck, *Developing Global Executives* (Boston: Harvard Business School Press, 2002).

[14]Harvard Longevity Study, "Harvard Study of Adult Development" and "Harvard Second Generation Study," Harvard (2015), www.adultdevelopmentstudy.org/.

[15]Larson, *The Splendid and the Vile.*

[16]Nancy Koehn, *Forged in Crisis: The Making of Five Courageous Leaders* (New York: Scribner Books, 2017), 234.

[17]Henry Kissinger, *Leadership: Six Studies in World Strategy* (New York: Penguin Press, 2022), xxiii.

[18]Kissinger, *Leadership*, 2-48.

[19]Kissinger, *Leadership*, 124-203.

[20]Kissinger, *Leadership*, 278-320.

[21]Kissinger, *Leadership*, 322-94.

[22]Kissinger, *Leadership*, 401.

[23]Alexis De Tocqueville, *Democracy in America*, trans. Harvey C. Mansfield and Delba Winthrop (Chicago: University of Chicago Press, 2000), 522.

[24]Winston Churchill, *Churchill's History of the English-Speaking Peoples* (New York: Dodd, Mead and Company, Inc., 1955, 1958). Arranged in one volume by Henry Steele Commager.

[25]Robert A. Emmons and Michael E. McCullough, "Counting Blessings Versus Burdens: An Experimental Investigation of Gratitude and Subjective Well-Being in Daily Life," *Journal of Personality and Social Psychology* 84, no. 2 (2003): 377-89.

[26]Tirel, "Why It's so Important to be Resilient."

[27]Hugo Huijer, "The Powerful Relationship Between Gratitude and Happiness," *Tracking Happiness* (January 2023), www.trackinghappiness.com/how-does-gratitude-make-us-happier-with-actual-examples.

[28]Richard Foster and Gayle D. Beebe, *Longing for God: Seven Paths of Christian Devotion* (Downers Grove, IL: InterVarsity Press, 2009). In the book, we identify the seven paths as: the right ordering of our love for God, journey, recovery of knowledge of God lost in the fall, intimacy with Jesus Christ, right ordering of our experiences of God, action and contemplation, and divine ascent.

THREE: THE CRUCIBLE OF HUMAN TREACHERY

[1]Dante Alighieri, *The Divine Comedy: The Inferno, The Purgatorio, and The Paradiso*, trans. John Ciardi (New York: Berkley Books, 2003).

[2]Josiah Royce, *The Basic Writings of Josiah Royce: Logic, Loyalty, and Community*, ed. John J. McDermott (New York: Fordham University Press, 2005).

[3]"Community Life Statement," Westmont College, accessed August 28, 2023, www.westmont.edu/about/community-commitments/community-life-statement.

[4]Plato, *The Republic*, trans. Sir Henry Desmond Pritchard Lee (New York: Penguin Publishing Group, 2007).

[5]Stanley Rachman, "Betrayal: A Psychological Analysis," National Library of Medicine, December 24, 2009, https://pubmed.ncbi.nlm.nih.gov/20035927/12-26-2022.

[6]Edwin H. Friedman, *Generation to Generation: Family Process in Church and Synagogue* (New York: Guilford Press, 1985).

[7]Edwin H. Friedman, *Failure of Nerve: Leadership in the Age of the Quick Fix* (New York: Seabury/Church Publishing, 2007).

[8]George Simon, *The Judas Syndrome* (Nashville: Abingdon Press, 2013).

[9]See Erin Meyer, *The Culture Map* (New York: PublicAffairs Books, 2014) for a more complete description of what is meant by "reading the air," which is essentially the

capacity to read the non-verbal elements that are a part of all human interaction and lend nuance and meaning to our human interactions.

[10]Friedman, *Failure of Nerve*, 133.

[11]Friedman, *Failure of Nerve*, 209.

[12]Robert Kegan and Lisa Laskow Lahey, *How the Way We Talk Can Change the Way We Work: Seven Languages for Transformation* (Hoboken, NJ: Jossey-Bass, 2000).

[13]Daniel Kahneman, *Thinking, Fast and Slow* (New York: Farrar, Straus and Giroux, 2013).

FOUR: THE CRUCIBLE OF AWAKENED MORAL CONSCIENCE

[1]Simone Weil, *Gravity and Grace* (Philadelphia: Routledge, 2002). Also: Simone Weil, *On Science, Necessity, and the Love of God* (London: Oxford University Press, 1968), 151-2.

[2]Clayborne Carson, *The Autobiography of Martin Luther King, Jr.* (London, UK: Abacus, 2000).

[3]James Stewart, *Heralds of God: A Practical Book on Preaching* (Vancouver, BC: Regent College Publishing, 1946).

[4]Reinhold Niebuhr, *Moral Man and Immoral Society: A Study in Ethics and Politics* (Louisville, KY: Westminster John Knox Press, 2013).

[5]Aretha Franklin, "Address at the Freedom Rally in Cobo Hall," June 23, 1963.

[6]Clayborne Carson, *A Call to Conscience: The Landmark Speeches of Dr. Martin Luther King, Jr.* (New York: Grand Central Publishing, 2002), 219-20. Martin Luther King Jr., "I've Been to the Mountaintop Speech," April 3, 1968.

[7]Martin Luther King Jr., "Nobel Peace Prize Acceptance Speech," December 10, 1964.

[8]Carson, *A Call to Conscience*, 165-7. Martin Luther King Jr., "Where Do We Go from Here? Speech," August 16, 1967.

[9]Carson, *A Call to Conscience*, 219-20.

[10]Max DePree, *Leadership Is An Art* (New York: Doubleday Business, 1989), 11.

[11]The most prominent and sustained engagement of Quakers with King came through various projects sponsored by the AFSC, the Quaker humanitarian organization that paid for the printing of his "Letters from a Birmingham Jail," provided funding for the "March on Washington" and the "Poor People's March," helped to underwrite his trip to India to visit sites of significance in the life of Gandhi, and nominated him for the Nobel Peace Prize in 1964, which he won.

[12]Carson, *A Call to Conscience*, 115. Martin Luther King Jr., "Speech following the March from Selma to Montgomery," March 25, 1965.

[13]Josiah Royce, *The Basic Writings of Josiah Royce: Logic, Loyalty, and Community*, ed. John J McDermott (New York: Fordham University Press, 2005).

14Carson, *A Call to Conscience*. Martin Luther King Jr., "Beyond Vietnam Speech," April 4, 1967.

15Carson, *A Call to Conscience*, 111-32. Introduction to "Address at the Conclusion of the Selma to Montgomery March" by John R. Lewis.

16Carson, *A Call to Conscience*, 116. Martin Luther King Jr., "March from Selma to Montgomery Speech," March 25, 1965.

17Clayborne Carson, *A Knock at Midnight: Inspiration from the Great Sermons of Reverend Martin Luther King, Jr.* (Brentwood, TN: Warner Books, 2000), 50. Martin Luther King Jr., "Loving Your Enemies Speech," November 17, 1957.

18Carson, *A Call to Conscience*, 191. Martin Luther King Jr., "Where Do We Go from Here? Speech," August 8, 1967.

19Reinhold Niebuhr, *The Children of Light and the Children of Darkness* (Chicago: The University of Chicago Press, 1944), xxxii.

20*The Simone Weil Reader,* ed. George A. Panichas (New York: Davi McKay Company, Inc., 1977), 9.

21Dietrich Bonhoeffer, *The Cost of Discipleship* (New York: Macmillan Publishing Co., 1937), 47.

FIVE: THE CRUCIBLE OF SOCIAL CONFLICT

1"Saints Among Us," *Time* magazine, December 29, 1975, https://time.com/vault/issue/1975-12-29/page/54/.

2George Yancey, *Neither Jew Nor Gentile: Exploring Issues of Racial Diversity on Protestant College Campuses* (New York: Oxford University Press, 2010).

3George Yancey, presentation via Zoom to the Westmont College Board of Trustees, January 29, 2021.

4George Yancey, *Beyond Racial Division: A Unifying Alternative to Colorblindness and Antiracism* (Downers Grove, IL: InterVarsity Press, 2022).

5Robert D. Putnam and Shaylyn Romney Garrett, *The Upswing: How America Came Together a Century Ago and How We Can Do It Again* (New York: Simon & Schuster, 2020).

6David Brooks, *The Road to Character* (New York: Random House Trade, 2016).

7Robert Bellah, William Sullivan, and Richard Madsen, *Habits of the Heart: Individualism and Commitment in American Life* (Berkeley: University of California Press, 1996).

8James Davidson Hunter, *To Change the World: The Irony, Tragedy, and Possibility of Christianity in the Late Modern World* (Oxford, UK: Oxford University Press, 2010).

9Jon Meacham, *His Truth Is Marching On: John Lewis and the Power of Hope* (New York: Random House, 2020).

[10]*John Lewis: Good Trouble* (film), CNN.com, accessed February 25, 2021, www.cnn .com/shows/john-lewis-good-trouble-cnn-film.

SIX: THE CRUCIBLE OF HUMAN SUFFERING

[1]Diogenes Allen, *Traces of God in a Frequently Hostile World* (Cambridge, MA: Cowley Publications, 1981).

[2]Harold Kushner, *When Bad Things Happen to Good People* (New York: Anchor Books, Random House, 1981).

[3]Walker Percy, *Lost In the Cosmos: The Last Self Help Book* (London, UK: Picador, 1985).

[4]Simone Weil, *Gravity and Grace* (Philadelphia: Routledge, 2002).

[5]Bernhard W. Anderson, *Out of the Depths: The Psalms Speak for Us Today* (Louisville, KY: Westminster Press, 1974).

[6]Elisabeth Kübler-Ross, *On Death and Dying: What the Dying Have to Teach Doctors, Nurses, Clergy and Their Own Families* (New York: Scribner, 2014). Kübler-Ross's is the best naturalistic explanation, which outlines the five stages of terminal illness leading to death: denial, anger, bargaining, depression, acceptance.

[7]Elie Wiesel, *Night* (New York: Hill and Wang, 1960).

[8]Viktor Frankl, *Man's Search for Meaning* (Boston: Beacon Press, 1959, 2006).

[9]Cynthia Gorney," The Power of Touch," National Geographic, June 2022. Tracy Dennis-Tiwary, PhD, *Future Tense: Why Anxiety Is Good for You Even Though It Feels Bad* (New York: Harper Wave, 2022).

[10]Blaise Pascal, *Pensées* (New York: Penguin, 1965 Krailsheimer edition), F149.

[11]Epictetus, *The Discourses of Epictetus: Books 1-4*, trans. George Long (Sioux Falls, SD: NuVision Publications, LLC, 2006).

SEVEN: THE CRUCIBLE OF PERSONAL CHOICE

[1]Meg Jay, *The Defining Decade: Why Your Twenties Matter and How to Make the Most of Them Now* (New York: Twelve, 2013).

[2]Daniel Kahneman, *Thinking, Fast and Slow* (New York: Farrar, Strauss and Giroux, 2011), 346-49.

[3]*Sophie's Choice*, directed by Alan J. Pakula (Universal Pictures, 1982).

[4]Soren Kierkegaard, *Either/Or: Part II*, ed. and trans. Howard V. Hong and Edna H. Hong (Princeton, NJ: Princeton University Press, 1988).

[5]Benedict Carey, "Brain Injury Said to Affect Moral Choices," *New York Times*, March 22, 2007, www.nytimes.com/2007/03/22/science/22brain.html.

[6]Jill Malik, Richard E. Heyman, and Amy M. Smith Slep, "Emotional Flooding in Response to Negative Affect in Couple Conflicts: Individual Differences and

Correlates," *American Psychological Association Journal of Family Psychology* (2019): https://doi.org/10.1037/fam0000584.

[7]Bruce McEwen, Carla Nasca, and Jason Gray, "Stress Effects on Neuronal Structure: Hippocampus, Amygdala, and Prefrontal Cortex," *Neuropsychopharmacology Reviews* 41 (2016): 3-13. Judith E. Glaser and Ross Tartell, "Conversational Intelligence at Work," *OD Practitioner* 46, no. 3 (2014).

[8]See Daniel Goleman, *Emotional Intelligence: Why It Can Matter More Than IQ* (New York: Random House Publishing, 2005), and Daniel Goleman, *Working with Emotional Intelligence* (New York: Bantam Books, 2000).

[9]Andrew Newberg and Mark Robert Waldman, *How God Changes Your Brain* (New York: Ballantine Books, 2010).

[10]Cynthia D. McCauley and Morgan W. McCall Jr., eds., *Using Experience to Develop Leadership Talent: How Organizations Leverage On-the-Job Development* (San Francisco: Jossey-Bass, 2014).

[11]Morgan W. McCall Jr. and George P. Hollenbeck, *Developing Global Executives* (Boston: Harvard Business School Press, 2002).

CONCLUSION: WISDOM FOR THE JOURNEY

[1]Nancy Koehn, *Forged in Crisis: The Making of Five Courageous Leaders* (New York: Scribner Books, 2017).

[2]David Brooks, *The Second Mountain: The Quest for a Moral Life* (New York: Random House, 2019).

[3]Brooks, *The Second Mountain*, 53.

[4]Saint Augustine, *The City of God*, trans. Marcus Dods (New York: The Modern Library, 1950).

[5]Jon Meacham, *His Truth Is Marching On: John Lewis and the Power of Hope* (New York: Random House, 2020).

FURTHER READING

BOOKS

Beebe, Gayle. *The Shaping of an Effective Leader: Eight Formative Principles of Leadership.* Downers Grove, IL: InterVarsity Press, 2011.

Black, Amy E. *Beyond Left and Right: Helping Christians Make Sense of American Politics.* Ada, MI: Baker Books, 2008.

Bonhoeffer, Dietrich. *The Cost of Discipleship.* New York: Macmillan, 1937.

Bonhoeffer, Dietrich. *Ethics.* Chicago: Touchstone, 1995.

Duhigg, Charles. *Smarter Faster Better: The Transformative Power of Real Productivity.* New York: Random House, 2017.

Carson, Clayborne. *Malcolm X: The FBI File.* New York: Skyhorse, 2012.

Carson, Clayborne, Emma J. Lapsansky-Werner, and Gary B. Nash. *The Struggle For Freedom: A History of African Americans, Volume 1, To 1877.* New York: Pearson, 2014.

Carson, Clayborne, Emma J. Lapsansky-Werner, and Gary B. Nash. *The Struggle For Freedom: A History of African Americans, Volume 2, Since 1865.* New York: Pearson, 2014.

Eig, Jonathan. *King: A Life.* New York: Farrar, Straus, and Giroux, 2023.

Foster, Richard, and Gayle D. Beebe. *Longing for God: Seven Paths of Christian Devotion.* Downers Grove, IL: InterVarsity Press, 2009.

Friedman, Edwin H. *A Failure of Nerve: Leadership in the Age of the Quick Fix.* New York: Church Publishing Inc, 2017.

Goodloe, Marcus "Goodie." *King Maker: Applying Dr. Martin Luther King Jr.'s Leadership Lessons in Working With Athletes and Entertainers.* Redondo Beach, CA: Dream Life Loud LLC, 2021.

Ince, Irwin L., Jr. *The Beautiful Community: Unity, Diversity, and the Church at Its Best.* Downers Grove, IL: InterVarsity Press, 2020.

Kahneman, Daniel. *Thinking, Fast and Slow.* New York: Farrar, Straus and Giroux, 2013.

Kendi, Ibram X. *How to Be an Antiracist.* London, UK: One World Publications, 2023.

King, Martin Luther, Jr. *The Autobiography of Martin Luther King, Jr.* Edited by Clayborne Carson. London, UK: Abacus, 2000.

King, Martin Luther, Jr., Clayborne Carson, and Kris Shepard, *A Call to Conscience: The Landmark Speeches of Dr. Martin Luther King, Jr.* New York: Grand Central Publishing, 2002.

Kissinger, Henry. *Leadership: Six Studies in World Strategy.* New York: Penguin Press, 2022.

Kotz, Nick. *Judgment Days: Lyndon Baines Johnson, Martin Luther King, Jr., and the Laws That Changed America*. Boston: Mariner Books, 2005.

Kuhn, Thomas. *The Structure of Scientific Revolutions*. Chicago: University of Chicago Press, 1996, 2012.

McCauley, Cynthia D. and Morgan W. McCall Jr., editors. *Using Experience to Develop Leadership Talent: How Organizations Leverage On-the-Job Development*. San Francisco: Jossey-Bass, 2014.

Putnam, Robert D., and Shaylyn Romney Garrett. *The Upswing: How America Came Together a Century Ago and How We Can Do It Again*. New York: Simon & Schuster, 2020.

Reynolds, Michael. *Still Off-Base About Race: When We Know The Truth, Things Will Be Different*. Stockbridge, GA: Dream Releaser Enterprises, 2021.

Romero, Robert Chao. *Brown Church: Five Centuries of Latina/o Social Justice, Theology, and Identity*. Downers Grove, IL: IVP Academic, 2020.

Steinbeck, John. *East of Eden*. New York: Penguin Books, 2002.

Steinbeck, John. *Cannery Row*. New York: Penguin Books, 1993.

Washington, Booker T. *Up From Slavery*. Garden City, NY: Dover Publications, 1995.

Weil, Simone. *The Simone Weil Reader*. Edited by George A Panichas. New York: David McKay Company, Inc., 1977.

Yancey, George. *Neither Jew Nor Gentile: Exploring Issues of Racial Diversity on Protestant College Campuses*. New York: Oxford University Press, 2010.

Yancey, George, and Ashlee Quosigk. *One Faith No Longer: The Transformation of Christianity in Red and Blue America*. New York: NYU Press, 2021.

DIGITAL RESOURCES

American Friends Service Committee. "AFSC's History with Rev. Dr. Martin Luther King's Poor People's Campaign." April 26, 2023. https://afsc.org/newsroom/afscs-history-rev-dr-martin-luther-kings-poor-peoples-campaign.

American Friends Service Committee. "From India to Birmingham: Martin Luther King, Jr.'s Connections with AFSC." March 30, 2010.

Bonanno, George A, Chris R. Brewin, Krzysztof Kaniasty, and Annette M. La Greca. "Weighing the Costs of Disaster: Consequences, Risks, and Resilience in Individuals, Families, and Communities." Sage Journals, *Psychological Science in the Public Interest* 11, no. 1 (January 1, 2010): 1-49. https://journals.sagepub.com/doi/10.1177/1529100610387086.

Carey, Benedict. "Brain Injury Said to Affect Moral Choices." *New York Times*. March 22, 2007. www.nytimes.com/2007/03/22/science/22brain.html.

De Witte, Melissa. "Clayborne Carson: Looking Back at a Legacy." *Stanford News*. August 28, 2020. https://news.stanford.edu/2020/08/28/clayborne-carson-looking -back-legacy/.

De Witte, Melissa. "Stanford Historian and Martin Luther King Jr. Scholar Clayborne Carson Offers a Personal Perspective on King's Legacy." *Stanford News*. January 16, 2013. https://shc.stanford.edu/stanford-humanities-center/news /stanford-historian-and-martin-luther-king-jr-scholar-clayborne.

Doe, Raymond, Erastus Ndinguri, and Simone T. A. Phipps. "Emotional Intelligence: The Link to Success and Failure of Leadership." *Academy of Educational Leadership Journal* 19, no. 3 (2015). www.proquest.com/openview/8349c82e5967c45518e80f 72a0ee826a/1?pq-origsite=gscholar&cbl=38741.

Emmons, Robert A and Michael E. McCullough. "Counting Blessings Versus Burdens: An Experimental Investigation of Gratitude and Subjective Well-Being in Daily Life." *Journal of Personality and Social Psychology* 84, no. 2 (2003): 377-89. https:// greatergood.berkeley.edu/pdfs/GratitudePDFs/6Emmons-BlessingsBurdens.pdf.

Feder, Adriana, Eric J. Nestler and Dennis S. Charney. "Psychobiology and Molecular Genetics of Resilience." National Library of Medicine. June, 2009. www .ncbi.nlm.nih.gov/pmc/articles/PMC2833107/.

Harrington, John. "The Most Famous Traitors in History." *24/7 Wall Street*. May 1, 2023. https://247wallst.com/special-report/2023/05/01/historys-famous-traitors/.

Holzel, Britta K., James Carmody, Karleyton C. Evans, Elizabeth A. Hogue, Jeffrey A. Dusek, Lucas Morgan, Roger K. Pitman, and Sarah W. Lazar. "Stress Reduction Correlates with Structural Changes in the Amygdala." *Social Cognitive and Affective Neuroscience* 5, no. 1 (2010): 11-17. https://academic.oup.com/scan/article /5/1/11/1728269.

Huijer, Hugo. "Happiness On A Scale From 1 To 10: How To + Implications." *Tracking Happiness*. January 2023. www.trackinghappiness.com/happiness-scale -from-1-to-10/.

Huijer, Hugo. "The Powerful Relationship Between Gratitude and Happiness." *Tracking Happiness*. January 2023. www.trackinghappiness.com/how-does-gratitude -make-us-happier-with-actual-examples.

King, Martin Luther, Jr., "I Have a Dream." in "March on Washington for Jobs and Freedom; Part 17 of 17," August 28, 1963, GBH Archives, accessed October 9, 2023, http://openvault.wgbh.org/catalog/A_76C3B93B557D4976A032C27C72AC ED18.

Tirel, Maili. "Why It's so Important to be Resilient: 3 Tips to Practice Resiliency." *Tracking Happiness*. January, 2023. www.trackinghappiness.com/importance-of -resilience.